# WIKILEAKS

# WIKILEAKS

## NEWS IN THE NETWORKED ERA

CHARLIE BECKETT WITH
JAMES BALL

polity

The right of Charlie Beckett and James Ball to be identified as Author of
this Work has been asserted in accordance with the UK Copyright, Designs
and Patents Act 1988.

First published in 2012 by Polity Press
Reprinted 2012

Polity Press
65 Bridge Street
Cambridge CB2 1UR, UK

Polity Press
350 Main Street
Malden, MA 02148, USA

ISBN-13: 978-0-7456-5975-6
ISBN-13: 978-0-7456-5976-3 (paperback)

A catalogue record for this book is available from the British Library.

Typeset in 10.75 on 14 pt Janson
by Servis Filmsetting Ltd, Stockport, Cheshire
Printed and bound in Great Britain by the MPG Books Group

The publisher has used its best endeavours to ensure that the URLs for
external websites referred to in this book are correct and active at the time
of going to press. However, the publisher has no responsibility for the
websites and can make no guarantee that a site will remain live or that the
content is or will remain appropriate.

Every effort has been made to trace all copyright holders, but if any have
been inadvertently overlooked the publisher will be pleased to include any
necessary credits in any subsequent reprint or edition.

For further information on Polity, visit our website: www.politybooks.com

# CONTENTS

# PREFACE

*Emily Bell*

When transparency organization WikiLeaks announced it held a vast trove of leaked US diplomatic cables in November 2010 it provoked a global political and journalistic maelstrom. In a digitized age of data capture and dissemination, where vast amounts of information can be published and shared among networks of citizens and activists without the mediation of the press, WikiLeaks raises fundamental questions about journalism, its processes and its role in a modern society.

For some, the work of Julian Assange, WikiLeaks editor-in-chief, and his collaborators, represented a remaking of the digital fourth estate which enjoyed none of the compromised closeness of relations between power and the press. For others it bordered on a terrorist organization, using its lack of accountability and its wide network of technologically capable followers to disrupt the orderly running of society. Wherever you sit on this spectrum of opinion, it is undeniable that the leaked cables, and the previous work of WikiLeaks, deserve close and proper examination. WikiLeaks' roots, its development and the consequences of its actions provide lessons for journalism, for regulators, for governments and for citizens. This timely book by Charlie Beckett and James Ball does not try to encompass all aspects of this sprawling narrative but wisely focuses on the portion most relevant to journalism.

What followed the sensational publication of the largest cache of confidential government documents in history was a dust cloud thrown up by the myriad of organizations rushing either to negate or to build on the extraordinary disclosures. Some of the questions which dominated debate at the time – such as 'is WikiLeaks journalism?' – obscured the more complicated questions about what the coming of age of this alternative media actually means. Up to this point, many of the technological changes being wrought on the media industry were interpreted principally in terms of how they affected business models. The key issues of what technological progress enables, and the types of organization it favours, were largely lost. The rhizomatic nature of WikiLeaks, its technical capabilities, its stateless structure provide a strong illustration of what type of organization can be supported by this new ecosystem. Mainstream media were confronted with an entity which outstripped their capacity to analyse and host documentation, which adopted a more liberal, even libertarian attitude to privacy, championed a radical transparency agenda and attracted support from many who saw the established press as inadequate and failing.

In tackling both the historical context of WikiLeaks and examining the ongoing questions that it raises, Charlie Beckett and James Ball provide us with a valuable framework for thinking about the wider future of journalism, disclosure and public information. As the book notes, without a geographic location and lying outside national legal jurisdictions, WikiLeaks has an 'unreplicated legal freedom, but also a less-reported but similarly liberating degree of ethical and moral flexibility'. The book takes a dispassionate look at the chronology of events and adds an analytical dimension to the story.

As the authors state : 'The challenge for government and the news media is how to cope with the variable geometry of journalism and regulation on the Internet.'

The vivid illustration WikiLeaks provides of the old adage that regulation can never keep pace with technology is accompanied by the darker truth outlined by many leading thinkers in this area that journalistic freedoms are not a given in the new networked environment. In fact, as the book outlines, the opposite might be true. We saw how, through withdrawal of platform and payment services from corporate providers, WikiLeaks was thrown back onto the power of the network to continue publishing. When the infrastructure which supports journalism is owned entirely by companies which at their heart are free of a journalistic mission, the consequences are troubling and potentially threatening for the operation of a free press.

The relationship between media and their audience, journalism and its subjects, government and transparency are all in a state of enforced renegotiation. WikiLeaks' abrupt and destabilizing intervention is one which will inform these ongoing discussions for a generation. It is heartening that authors with the insight of Beckett and Ball should be helping to frame and guide this discussion at a time when the issues are still vital and alive.

# INTRODUCTION

WikiLeaks is the most challenging journalism phenomenon to emerge in the digital era. The stories it has broken have been compared to historic scoops such as the Pentagon Papers that revealed that President Johnson's administration had lied about the conduct of the Vietnam War. The model it created is a radical development in journalism story-telling on a par with the creation of a new genre like blogging. It has provoked anger and enthusiasm in equal measures, from across the political and journalistic spectrum. WikiLeaks poses a series of challenges to the status quo in politics, journalism and theories of political communications. It has compromised the foreign policy operations of the most powerful state in the world. It has caused the most mighty news organizations to collaborate with this relatively tiny editorial outfit. Yet it may also be on the verge of extinction.

Its use of new technologies and the way it puts information into the public domain forces us to reconsider what journalism is and its moral purpose in contemporary global politics. What are the responsibilities of a journalist? What are the limits on freedom of expression? What are the best forms for political media in the Internet age? How far does the public's 'right to know' extend?

WikiLeaks is inherently unstable as a concept and a practice. It has changed over its decade-long life. Its very name suggests a kind of open, participatory activity that it has never properly realized. Indeed, its current direction is taking it ever further from the Wiki model. At the time of writing it is on the threshold of a new phase that might bring expansion or dissolution. The status of its founder Julian Assange is subject to legal challenge at a personal level as well as for WikiLeaks' actions as a whole. Other similar organizations have now sprung up around the world, with versions also emerging in mainstream media. So, as with so many online innovators before it, WikiLeaks' real significance may be what follows in its wake, rather than its short, turbulent history.*

WikiLeaks has deliberately resisted easy definition. There has always been a gulf between what the world thought WikiLeaks was and the reality. Assange and his associates often encouraged this discrepancy, as they were always keen to exaggerate the resources and potential of the organization. Mainstream journalists were surprisingly keen to accept the more dramatic representation. At times media coverage of WikiLeaks made it look like SPECTRE, the evil secret empire in the James Bond films, with Assange as Blofeld, commanding armies of radical data-journalists ready to bring

---

* See the Epilogue of this book for a summary of the latest and highly significant development at the end of August 2011 when WikiLeaks released all the Embassy cables in full, causing condemnation from former mainstream media partners and a bitter row over the editorial ethics and organizational direction of WikiLeaks amongst supporters and critics.

down Western Democracy with one push of a red 'publish' button. In fact, it was a ramshackle, ad hoc organization that often struggled to stay online.

When examined critically, WikiLeaks itself is not a revolutionary idea. It is best seen as a radical new hybrid combining 'hacktavism' with some of the traits of more traditional investigative journalism. In the end, its challenge to orthodoxy might reside in its extra-legal status rather than the rather vague anti-hegemonic world-view of Assange and his associates. Its cross-national servers and network of thousands of 'mirrored' sites duplicating its content have created a new kind of publisher of last resort.

WikiLeaks should be seen as a significant part of the current reshaping of the fourth estate. It is a prototype for the shift from a closed, linear structure to a more open, networked and collaborative process. Information flows are changing. Control over what the public knows is being exercised and resisted in new ways. The traditional model for the relationship between authority, media and citizen is no longer sustainable. Of course, that does not mean that power will inevitably be redistributed in a more equitable or transparent way. But WikiLeaks is one of many new forms of political communications that offer new opportunities for a reshaping of democratic discourse and, potentially at least, of politics itself.

This book is a collaboration between two journalists. Charlie Beckett had a conventional mainstream media career and now runs Polis, a think-tank that acts as a forum for public debate about journalism and a centre for research into contemporary international news media at the London School of Economics. James Ball worked for WikiLeaks and is now an investigative journalist specializing in data at the *Guardian* newspaper in Britain. We aim to describe the history of WikiLeaks in terms of its significance for journalism, both as an evolving practice and in relation to its wider theoretical and conceptual context. We will explain why WikiLeaks matters for anyone interested in news media: as practitioners, consumers or analysts.

This is not a definitive 'insider' account or a detailed history of WikiLeaks, though it will give the essential chronology. The story is by no means over, so inevitably we are describing a narrative that is constantly developing beyond the date of publication of this book. Nor is it a biographical analysis of Julian Assange – although it is impossible to separate his personality and career from WikiLeaks generally. Instead, it will situate the meaning of WikiLeaks and its history in relation to its wider impact and importance. We will look at WikiLeaks as a particular phenomenon but also as part of a wide-ranging phase of journalism reconstruction, innovation and change.

The book is set out in four chapters. Each one first tells the story and then describes the meaning of WikiLeaks at that point in its history. Each section looks at a different period of WikiLeaks: the creation and early phase; the major Afghan, Iraq and Embassy cable leaks; the legal battle and struggle for survival; and finally an examination of the future for WikiLeaks and its significance in the context of emerging forms of political communication. Each chapter will start with a brief introduction to the themes, followed by a substantial narrative that will set out the key events. Then there will be a discussion of the significance of WikiLeaks' activities in that period and an analysis of its nature and impact.

So in the first section we examine where WikiLeaks comes from and the landscape into which it emerged. We will trace its roots in the 'hacktavist' campaigners who sought to penetrate into closed corporate or governmental information systems to extract data. Some hackers did this for the challenge, for profit or for fun, but others because they had political goals. Assange was personally connected into a loose network of 'cypherpunk' computer activists who shared technological information, but who also conducted a lively conversation about the ethics of the Internet. This was the period for which we have early written evidence of Julian Assange's ideological outlook. We can see how WikiLeaks itself is set up on 4 October 2006 with the 'whistle-blower' model. As well as technical problems in terms of storage, processing and security, there are immediately legal and ethical issues that arise, partly because of the special nature of WikiLeaks as a platform for disclosure.

One of its first stories, the revelations about the widespread nature of corruption in Kenya's national elite, for example, showed how it was able to exploit its trans-national status to override state controls in order to put highly controversial information into the public domain. It could publish an explosive secret report that Kenyan media did not have access to or did not feel able to make public for fear of reprisal. Within a year, it replicated this feat in the Western world, publishing a report on the British oil company Trafigura that the UK media were barred from reporting due to legal restrictions.

WikiLeaks was briefly shut down by an injunction after it published details of the alleged illegal activities of a branch of a Swiss bank. But through a process of 'mirrored' websites created by supporters it was, in effect, able to be damned and to publish. The injunction was eventually overturned but WikiLeaks had shown and would continue to demonstrate that it was able to operate with impunity. It has no home base and no legal entity in any one country and so effectively had become what Jay Rosen called the world's 'first' stateless media organization.[1] While Assange was living out of a suitcase, WikiLeaks was living in cyberspace. It had its best-known physical servers in Sweden, but its networks of supporters meant it existed everywhere and nowhere.

We will then analyse what is new about WikiLeaks in this phase and in what ways it is a challenge to alternative media, to mainstream media and to power itself. First, we will examine how Assange's project fits into existing ideas of disruptive, non-traditional, non-commercial or unsubsidized news media. Is it a new form of counter-cultural, anti-hegemonic journalism? We argue that it begins as an evolving, protean form of alternative media. In its practice and structure it is self-consciously apart from mainstream media with a declared radical political outlook. It uses new technologies and novel organizational methods. It adapts but also rejects other alternative media paradigms.

It did have guiding principles: to protect sources, to publish everything. It is at this point that some of the core ethical questions arise. The most basic was how it could publish material that it did not know was genuine. Despite public statements to the contrary, documents were validated in a very informal way. Not everything that has been given to WikiLeaks has been published yet, but when it was, at this point in its history, it was published in full. In fact, throughout its history, no-one has ever successfully questioned the authenticity of any document published by WikiLeaks. But it is clear that in the initial stages, few of the more 'responsible' editorial checks and balances of mainstream media were observed at WikiLeaks.

WikiLeaks in this early phase was evolving, however, and in some ways towards a more recognizable model of journalism. The Collateral Murder video filmed by the crew of an American Apache helicopter as they shot a group of Iraqis – including two Reuters employees – was a seminal moment. WikiLeaks released all 39 minutes of the cockpit footage on YouTube. But they also released a highly edited version with subtitles, graphics and introductory statements. They commissioned two journalists, Kristinn Hrafnsson and Ingi Ingason Ragnar, to visit Iraq to interview victims' families. It was a highly partisan but recognizably journalistic documentary film.

We will see how this contrasts with mainstream journalism, which at that time was grappling with the implications of the new digital communications environment. Mainstream news media in the West are facing a business crisis as their sources of revenue are eroded by the Internet. At the same time new online news sources are emerging that offer information directly to the public for free, anytime they want it. Bloggers and social networks are also generating 'journalism' – usually for free – that is competing with their product. More fundamentally, the Internet is challenging the role of mainstream media in the mediation of politics. The way that traditional mass media framed political narratives and the issues that they chose to put on the agenda is being questioned afresh.

Then we will analyse how much of a challenge WikiLeaks was at this time to those in authority. Julian Assange had a world-view of power as a 'conspiracy' or network. This could be disrupted by breaking the control of those in authority over information. He argued that revelations of secret material would lead to political reaction by an outraged public. The Collateral Murder video release was the key test case of this theory. It made graphically visible the actions of power in a way that mainstream and alternative media had arguably failed to do. Yet, along with the other leaks in this period, it was not having the widespread political impact that Assange had hoped for. While reaction from the US administration was angry, there was no perceptible impact on either policy or public opinion. WikiLeaks now had a model and a strategy of sorts, but its effect was relatively limited.

The second chapter of this book will look at WikiLeaks as a much more potent challenge to power as well as to journalism. In 2010 the US Department of Defense paid WikiLeaks the compliment of a report outlining how to deter the website's activities. WikiLeaks obtained and published a leaked copy. It showed how significant WikiLeaks was now politically. The Department of Defense was proved more right to be worried than even they could have anticipated when WikiLeaks produced a series of disclosures that took its operations to an unprecedented scale. The Afghan war logs, the Iraq war logs and the Embassy cable leaks were the biggest acts of unauthorized information disclosure ever undertaken. Around 750,000 documents were involved, many of which have still to go through the publication process.

The sheer volume was important. It meant that, instead of a conventional one-off scoop, there has been a process of revelation. This makes it impossible for any one person to understand its full complexity. It may even have reduced the effect of individual disclosures by swamping the audience with a surplus of information. However, it has created a sustainable, continuing process of accountability that challenges the way power works as well as authority itself. It made visible – literally in the case of the video – the way that governments think and act away from media scrutiny. Many of the revelations had direct consequences, although the degree to which that happened has been debated. Specific revelations – such as the decision by the US to spy on UN officials – were substantial and new. Other information, such as the corruption of Tunisia's President, may have played a small role in that country's uprising in early 2011. Military and intelligence operations were allegedly compromised by WikiLeaks' revelations. Certainly, procedures around intelligence and information-sharing have been changed in response. Our understanding of the nature of war and diplomacy has been enhanced. Journalism's role as the provider of the first draft of history was deepened.

The extraordinary extent of these revelations exposed the relative failure of much of conventional media to hold power to account. Even without resorting to theories of manufactured consent, WikiLeaks made it clear that traditional journalism is severely limited in its scope. It is constrained by commercial, technical, legal and cultural boundaries that WikiLeaks was happy and able to cross. WikiLeaks demonstrated that investigative journalism could go much further using new technologies, especially when combined with what some of its mainstream media collaborators have described as intellectual and ethical 'recklessness'. This in turn challenges conventional liberal democratic notions of the settlement of power between media and politicians as a mutually responsible process.

At the same time WikiLeaks itself was becoming networked into mainstream media across the globe as it shifted from isolated whistle-blower to collaborative investigator and publisher. In this phase WikiLeaks can be seen to be an example of a 'Networked Journalism' organization. It uses disruptive techniques from citizen journalism and exploits the potential of the new data journalism. But it combines this with a partnership relationship with mainstream media organizations such as the *New York Times*, the *Guardian* and *Der Spiegel*. This process was, in fact, instigated by a traditional investigative journalist, Nick Davies of the *Guardian*. Despite objections on many issues by Julian Assange, the nature of the project was also extensively shaped by the mainstream media partners. This strained but effective relationship gave WikiLeaks access to mass audiences and the editorial resources of elite Western media.

We then analyse how WikiLeaks in this phase relates to ethical ideas about journalism. How does it conceive of its position in respect of the rights and responsibilities that are supposed to characterize the relationship of mainstream media to wider society? How does WikiLeaks deal with expectations that it will avoid harm, attempt to tell truth and hold power to account? This period of its greatest success also highlights some of the tensions and even contradictions inherent in WikiLeaks. For example, it was clear that the mainstream media journalists had quite different standards for redacting information that could have put people's lives at risk. According to the *Guardian*, 'They had it coming' was Assange's response to the prospect of Afghani informants being identified and targeted. In contrast, both Bill Keller (*New York Times*) and Alan Rusbridger (the *Guardian*) were prepared to talk to the authorities in advance, albeit in very general terms, about what was being published.

In the third chapter of the book, we look at the latest phase of WikiLeaks and what it means as a model for journalism. The arrest of Assange, the fight back by him and his supporters and the splits in WikiLeaks dominate the most recent narrative around WikiLeaks. A series of books have given different personal perspectives on what happened, but also some immediate judgements of its significance. Putting aside the personal issue of the legal process, the (almost) unravelling of WikiLeaks does tell us something about its inherent instability, but also its resilience.

By 2011 it had become almost entirely dependent upon one person. It was struggling to process, and even retain control of, the material it had, let alone to solicit new information. But it had survived an extraordinary onslaught. Apart from the personal legal issues for Assange, there were a series of structural attacks. A range of important American politicians called for the prosecution of WikiLeaks beyond the ongoing attempt to extradite Assange in connection with the leaking of US government documents. Corporations such as Amazon which provided server space refused to host WikiLeaks while PayPal, Mastercard and Visa all declined to provide payment services. WikiLeaks was affected but it survived. It continued to co-publish agenda-setting disclosures around the world, causing a major political scandal in India, for example. It also continued to co-publish with Western newspapers, such as the *Telegraph* in Britain.

Perhaps more important though is what the hostile reaction by the US government, banks and Internet companies says about the nature of the argument over the future of the Internet itself. That hostility to WikiLeaks has exposed a tension at the heart of American policy on global information flows and the role of the Internet and democracy. As Timothy Wu's *Master Switch* has suggested, we are at a defining moment where the Internet may evolve into a much more controlled space. WikiLeaks is a kind of test case for this thesis.

By examining the future of WikiLeaks and related media organizations we can understand its significance and also explore the potential evolution of journalism in the mature Internet age. WikiLeaks is a model. It has already spawned clones and variations that deploy similar whistle-blowing data techniques. It is part of a wider move from classic investigative journalism to a range of new organizations – often supported by activists or public and philanthropic funds. It is indicative of a new global civic environment where data are used as a political tool or weapon. Just when mainstream journalism may become faster and shallower, this trend offers the potential of deeper as well as more disruptive journalism. WikiLeaks has helped focus the debate about journalism in an age where classic ideas of objectivity are being supplemented by notions of accountability and interactivity.

In the fourth chapter, we will discuss WikiLeaks in the context of its future as an organization, but also in the much wider setting of networked political communications. We will compare it to the other trends, such as social media, that are evolving new forms of journalism and even redefining the idea of news itself. The journalism WikiLeaks represents appears to have a series of choices. It can attempt to remain outside mainstream politics and journalism as a model for alternative media: something that no other radical news organization has managed to sustain on any kind of scale, even in the Internet era. Or it can become networked into other media organizations and perhaps become a kind of new Networked (or Mutualized) News agency. Or it can become more of a transparency NGO, a digital Human Rights Watch for data. That would give it legitimacy and institutional influence. It would also bring WikiLeaks into the same media space of advocacy journalism that other NGOs are increasingly occupying. This will require a degree of soul-searching by an organization that sometimes appears not to understand exactly what its unique features are. Assange has suggested variously that these are its political ideology, its technologically driven impunity or its role as an agency for subversives and advocacy. Most recently he has placed it within the historical tradition of the radical press. Does it have the capacity for institutional self-reflection or is WikiLeaks' future subject to one man's wishes?

At the same time the wider context of political communications is changing. Across the world we see how communications are becoming disintermediated. The middle-man role of traditional journalists is being cut out. Individuals are now able to report their world directly and to create networks of communication apart from conventional news media. Cyber-optimists hope for a new era of transparency created by citizen-driven media. The example of the 2011 Arab uprisings suggests that this might go further and become a tool of political reform as well. We take time to analyse the significance of that episode as a contrast to the WikiLeaks model, albeit a potentially complementary trend. Social media allow so-called 'weak ties' to combine into an effective catalyst and channel for politically challenging communications. The low-cost, minimal effort acts of online media can combine into more powerful networked actions. Micro-blogging services like Twitter or video websites like YouTube do not cause, let alone complete, real-world revolutions, but they do seem to play a critical role in stimulating and amplifying the information that fuels the protests and enables their organization. Mainstream media are becoming more conscious of how they must engage with this social mediation by linking to and using these flows of imagery, information and opinion. The future for data disclosure websites like WikiLeaks is finding a place in this new ecology.

WikiLeaks has made us reconsider how politics and journalism work. It also makes us think again about the future of politics as well as of political journalism. But ultimately its real value may be to show that the very nature of journalism and news has changed. Political media once had a defined structure that created a limited product. They had quite a specific function in liberal democracies as the conduit of information between power and the people. The Internet and digital communications have the capacity to change that relationship. Something like WikiLeaks would have been literally impossible in the pre-Internet age. The scale of the leak, and the ability to spread it globally, are enabled by the new technology and the Net. But this is more than the underground dissident journalism or Samizdat of the Cold War period adapted for the digital era. WikiLeaks is a network exploit that uses the Internet in a radical way to gather material, to protect itself and to tap into other networks, including mainstream media. This allows it to communicate information in new ways. WikiLeaks' significance is that it is part of the shift in the nature of news to a process, a network system, that is contestable and unstable. Welcome to Wiki World and the era of uncertainty.

# 1

# WHAT WAS NEW ABOUT WIKILEAKS?

## 1.1 THE CREATION OF WIKILEAKS

WikiLeaks is no longer a Wiki. Indeed, Jimmy Wales, the founder of the online encyclopedia Wikipedia is somewhat irritated by the way their shared word-stems make people link the two organizations.[1] Wikipedia is a collaborative online information resource that is written and edited by volunteers. It has rules but it is an open-source, participatory production model. It is regularly cited as one of the digital age's greatest achievements.[2] It is also hailed as a triumph of the free Internet's ability to create an unprecedented resource out of networked knowledge and interactive connectivity.

Despite its name, WikiLeaks, as the world has now come to know it, does not operate in the same way. Back in 2008 the WikiLeaks 'Frequently Asked Questions' or 'FAQs' section did make the comparison:

WikiLeaks looks like Wikipedia. Anybody can post comments to it. No technical knowledge is required. Whistleblowers can post documents anonymously and untraceably. Users can publicly discuss documents and analyze their credibility and veracity. Users can discuss the latest material, read and write explanatory articles on leaks along with background material and context. The political relevance of documents and their veracity can be revealed by a cast of thousands.[3]

However, while in practice it moved away from this open-system model, it does share some of that conceptual grounding in the way it exploits the unique affordances of the World Wide Web. It could only exist thanks to the Internet. WikiLeaks founder Julian Assange and colleagues like Daniel Domscheit-Berg emerged from a 'hacker' culture, but WikiLeaks itself soon moved away from the idea of penetrating other people's systems. Much of its early material was alleged to have consisted of trawled files left on peer-to-peer networks, either unintentionally or as the result of system hacks. However, it soon became instead a safe haven for the produce of other people's deliberate 'whistle-blowing' to WikiLeaks: 'We don't have targets, other than organizations that use secrecy to conceal unjust behavior . . . that's created a general target. Otherwise we're completely source-dependent. We are a source-protection organization and a publishing-protection organization.'[4] As we look at the emergence of WikiLeaks we can see how it forged a particularly effective, though not unique, model as a kind of hybrid publisher of last resort.

In this first chapter, we will examine where WikiLeaks comes from and the landscape into which it emerged. We will trace its roots through the 'hacktavist' movements which sought to penetrate into closed corporate or governmental information systems to extract data. Much like smaller, more skilled versions of today's Anonymous network of computer activists, some hackers did this for the challenge, for profit or for fun, but others because they had political goals.[5] From these groups, the co-founders of what became WikiLeaks emerged.

Julian Assange is credited as the co-author of a 2001 book by technology researcher Suelette Dreyfus chronicling the hacktivist culture of the time. *Underground: Tales of Hacking, Madness, and Obsession on the Electronic Frontier*[6] featured the characters behind a series of hacks, including the defence and intelligence hacks carried out by 'Mendax', Assange's hacker alter-ego.

Characteristically, Julian Assange became convinced the book should be published online, in its entirety, for free. As the preface to the electronic edition shows, he got his way. '"Why would an author give away an unlimited number of copies of her book for free?" That's a good question', Dreyfus wrote; 'When "Underground"'s researcher, Julian Assange, first suggested releasing an electronic version of the book on the Net for free, I had to stop and think about just that question.'[7]

As Dreyfus explains, the book is a hackers' perspective of the electronic underground:

> Who are hackers? Why do they hack? There are no simple answers to these questions. Each hacker is different. To that end, I have attempted to present a collection of individual but interconnected stories. While each hacker has a distinct story, there are common themes which appear through-out many of the stories. Rebellion against all symbols of authority. Dysfunctional families. Bright children suffo-cated by ill-equipped teachers. Mental illness or instability. Obsession and addiction.[8]

This attempt to understand the psychological elements of the hacker culture does seem appropriate in the light of later developments regarding Assange's personal life and the dominant role his personality played in WikiLeaks' history. His character-forming upbringing, raised by his mother on her own, constantly changing homes and schools, mixing with an eclectic range of adults, helped to forge an Internet innovator. Suelette Dreyfus, the book's primary author, remains involved with Assange and with WikiLeaks, and is referred to as 'The Nanny' in Daniel Domscheit-Berg's account of his time with WikiLeaks.[9]

After his conviction for his hacking activities in Australia, Assange studied maths, physics, philosophy and neuroscience at the University of Melbourne, though he did not complete his studies. During this period, his ideas around leaking were becoming more solid. In 1999, a full seven years before the birth of WikiLeaks, Julian Assange registered the domain leaks.org. 'But', he told an interviewer, 'I didn't do anything with it.'[10] However, seven years later, the different strands of thinking began to coalesce, as Assange and others began discussing the formation of WikiLeaks.

WikiLeaks.org was registered in 4 October 2006, with its first material appearing two months later in December 2006. Alongside was the claim that it was 'founded by Chinese dissidents, journalists, mathematicians and start-up company technologists, from the US, Taiwan, Europe, Australia and South Africa'. As is often the case with WikiLeaks, the core team was actually a lot smaller than its public relations claimed. It consisted largely of Assange and individuals from the 'Chaos Computer Club', a German group of pro-transparency hackers.[11] WikiLeaks' claimed membership was rather larger than reality, and its initial impact was also more modest than its publicity had suggested.

The site claimed to have over 1 million documents ready

to leak. It launched with just one: a document purporting to be from an Islamic resistance group in Somalia, allegedly leaked via the Chinese government. A 'health warning' assessing the document's veracity was published alongside. It warned that WikiLeaks had been unable to verify completely whether the document was genuine or not, though it gave evidence why the site believed it to be genuine. WikiLeaks was not challenged on the veracity of the document by either the Chinese government or Somali groups.

Many of WikiLeaks' earliest plans at this stage were revealed – paradoxically – through leaked documents.[12] An email sent to early supporters and collaborators, for example, stated that the site planned to 'numerically eclipse the content of the english wikipedia with leaked documents'. The early users were political activists, promising to 'provide a catalyst which will bring down government through stealth everywhere, not least that of the Bushists'.[13]

Conversations within WikiLeaks revolved around the difficulty of verifying leaked documents and the need for honesty in analysis. The key internal debate was the struggle to remain collegiate and sustain ethical behaviour. Occasional comments look profoundly insightful in retrospect: 'We're on an exponential; we have no forces working against us yet, but there will be many in a few months and these early discussions may take on an unexpected poignancy.'[14]

Other key insights from the time come from John Young, the founder of the oldest well-known leaking website on the Internet: cryptome.org. Since 1996 Cryptome has accepted open submissions, and publishes documents largely unredacted and free of accompanying editorial, almost daily. Concentrating mainly on the fields of security and technology, it has never achieved the wider profile or controversial impact of WikiLeaks, despite featuring in many stories over the years.

Young, in whose name WikiLeaks.org was initially registered to protect the anonymity of other contributors, was often the voice of caution in the discussion threads:

> Leaks should be doubted and doubts answered by leakers or those who distribute the leakables. An iron-clad leak is a phony or a lie. It does require more work to perform an exegesis of a leaked document weighing the pros and cons, but that is what it takes to avoid the trap of vainglorious pride in being a leaker and the subsequent lure of leaking crap to remain in the spotlight – the politician's disease.[15]

WikiLeaks had a strong early claim to a pioneering role in the development of information security. Assange refers even now to the part he played in setting up hidden open-source encryption standards. These enable WikiLeaks and its sources to hold and disseminate information unreadable by anyone else in the world, including security services. WikiLeaks uses such protocols today in its publicly available, but heavily encrypted, 'insurance' file. This is the password to a package of information intended for release should anything untoward happen to Assange. The same security guards its other mechanisms such as its (offline at the time of writing) submissions system. Though WikiLeaks has often suffered its own leaks, and even on occasion lost control of its material, its encryption technology is sophisticated and effectively unbreakable. WikiLeaks uses a form of encryption known as 256-bit AES, similar to that used by online banking sites, and the military and intelligence agencies themselves. With a sufficiently strong and well-protected password, breaking in to such a file would take several million times longer than the lifespan of the universe.[16]

Such robust security precautions didn't mean the initial running of the site was entirely smooth. Even in 2007

– before most of the world had noticed the site existed – WikiLeaks had its first brush with internal dissent, and within the early months of 2008 the site had received its first major legal threat. The leaked emails quoted above are part of a huge document dump from WikiLeaks' earliest days, made by Cryptome's John Young. By January 2007, a WikiLeaker, believed to be Assange, had posted that 'it is our goal to raise pledges of $5m by July', a goal the site is still far from reaching. This declaration of financial ambition provoked a strong reaction from Young. He posted a series of warnings to the email list of WikiLeaks activists on the risks of such ambitious goals and rhetoric. 'Announcing a $5 million fund-raising goal by July will kill this effort. It makes WL appear to be a Wall Street scam. This amount could not be needed so soon except for suspect purposes', he wrote. Scepticism unleashed, he continued:

I'd say the same about the alleged 1.1 million documents ready for leaking. Way too many to be believable without evidence. I don't believe the number. So far, one document, of highly suspect provenance.

Instead, explain what funding needs there are and present a schedule for their need, avoid generalities and lump sums. Explain how the funds will be managed and protected against fraud and theft. The biggest crooks brag overmuch of how ethical their operations are. Avoid ethical prom-ises, period, they've been used too often to fleece victims. Demonstrate sustained ethical behavior, don't preach/ peddle it.

In another comment posted just twenty minutes later, Young concluded WikiLeaks was a 'fraud'. He then pub-lished the anonymized contents of the WikiLeaks mailing list on his own site. Two years later, a non-anonymized version of WikiLeaks' 108-strong donors' list was again leaked, this time as a result of an email error by Assange himself. The teething troubles did not slow WikiLeaks' momentum, or revelations. One of WikiLeaks' first stories, exposing widespread corruption in Kenya's elite, for example, showed how it was able to exploit its transnational status to override state controls and to put highly controversial information into the public domain. WikiLeaks had published a confidential report produced by a UK security intelligence company, Kroll Associates, in April 2004, into corruption in Kenya.[17] It found the still-influential former President of Kenya had laundered public money to buy property overseas in the UK, New York, South Africa and Australia. The revelations were linked – by Assange at least – to the riots and civil unrest which accompanied the December 2007 elections in the country: '1,300 people were eventually killed, and 350,000 were displaced. That was a result of our leak ... On the other hand, the Kenyan people had a right to that information and 40,000 children a year die of malaria in Kenya. And many more die of money being pulled out of Kenya, and as a result of the Kenyan shilling being debased.'[18]

With this leak, WikiLeaks had shown it could publish an explosive secret report that Kenyan media did not have access to or did not feel able to make public for fear of reprisal. It also indicated that WikiLeaks, and Assange in particular, were prepared to make a different risk calculation that accepted some incidental harm for the 'greater good' of transparency. Regardless of the degree to which WikiLeaks did substantially influence events in reality, the Kenyan leaks were very much a herald of things to come.

So, not surprisingly, its targets were now fighting back. WikiLeaks has only once been taken offline through legal action, and never for longer than 24 hours by technical means. Swiss bank Julius Baer, in a February 2008 action, managed to injunct Dynadot, the US company hosting the site's DNS servers. This was the service which routed users from the WikiLeaks.org web address to WikiLeaks' European-hosted servers.

As UK celebrities have since found, however, injunctions are a risky business. Web forums, blogs and other users were quick to point to the direct IP address to WikiLeaks, and to other web addresses effectively linking to the information that the bank had sought to suppress. Within a month of the original injunction being issued, the Julius Baer bank had dropped their case and the site was reinstated and normal WikiLeaks service resumed.

Julius Assange is proud to report, as a result of this and other, lesser, ultimately unsuccessful legal challenges to the site, that the organization has never lost a courtroom battle. But Dynadot was correctly identified as a weak link in the WikiLeaks chain. Two years later, when US Senator Joe Lieberman called on American companies to boycott WikiLeaks, the loss of Amazon's web servers took the site offline for mere hours. The loss of Dynadot forced the WikiLeaks.org website to move to the WikiLeaks.ch web address for several months before the original domain name was recovered in May 2011.

So what was new about WikiLeaks in its first two years? Above all, it had shown and would continue to demonstrate that it was able to operate with impunity. It had no home base and was not a legal entity in any one country. In effect it had become a stateless media organization.[19] While Assange was living out of a suitcase, WikiLeaks was living in cyberspace. Its physical servers may have been in Sweden or Germany, but its networks of supporters and mirrored sites meant it existed everywhere and nowhere. This is fundamentally different from traditional news media. Conventional

mass media's whole relationship to power and its ethical
framework is conditioned by the fact that they can be held
to account by national and international regulations and
laws. Even in the most free-market and open self-regulatory
media systems, these apply. In many ways, WikiLeaks is
much more a legal revolution in contemporary media than a
technological one.

In addition to the legal constraints, there are other
responsibilities or restrictions on journalism that are nor-
mally part of the trade-off between freedom of expression
and the rights of wider society to privacy and fair representation. These include cultural assumptions about a sense of
'fair play' or balance and accuracy in reporting. These are
widely abused and hugely variable from one media outlet or
market to another – even within Western liberal democracies. But they exist and they characterize mainstream news
media as an information system with codes of behaviour
that are internally constructed as well as externally enforced.
From them flow ideas such as 'objectivity', a concept itself
with different interpretations from nation to nation. Around
them are created the kind of media institutions that protect
these ideas, sustain these cultures and gather the resources to
deliver the product they create. These may vary in practice
from the public-sector bodies like the BBC to the corporate, such as Fox News. But from *The Times* in New York
or London to *The Times* in Brownsville, Oregon, the mainstream news organizations have in common a physical, social
and legal presence. By escaping from the constraints of law
and location, WikiLeaks accessed a much greater potential
freedom. Impunity from law gives it immunity from the consequences of the wider settlement between journalism and
society. This grants WikiLeaks unprecedented and, so far,
unreplicated legal freedom, but also a less-reported but similarly liberating degree of ethical and moral flexibility.

Yet, in many other respects, WikiLeaks in this first phase has the characteristics of conventional journalism. The idea of a leaker, for example, is as old as journalism itself. Those sending material to WikiLeaks may have been using new technologies such as encryption or, more prosaically, email. Certainly, Bradley Manning allegedly exploited the weakness of an incredibly powerful digital information system. The technology allowed leaks of unprecedented scale but the motives and actions are timeless. The methodology and morality were typical of whistle-blowing to journalists throughout media history. It usually takes something quite exceptional to make someone betray the trust of their employers or associates. It can be personal or political, petty or principled. The news media have always relied on it and most journalism regulatory systems make special allowance for the public interest justification of breaking the law, or at least of publishing the results of what is often a crime.

Like traditional mainstream media, WikiLeaks also had an editor and a newsroom – of sorts – that processed the information. In later stages, they would edit and package the material too. Even with unedited material there is a degree of contextualization of most of the important leaks. The Kenyan leak, for example, has an introduction written by 'WikiLeaks staff' that gives a political context for the document. It also gives links to sources that help establish its veracity and even asserts a motive for the leak itself: 'The leak which emanated from within high levels of the Kenyan Government is motivated by the desire to demonstrate that President Kibaki has clear-cut evidence of his predecessor's corruption and complicity in corruption, and has chosen to suppress the evidence and worse still has gone into a political and economic alliance with the Moi group.'[20]

So, from its 'pure' Wiki construct, we see in this phase how the organization is constantly evolving in the direction

of traditional newsroom practice. This is at a time coinciden-
tally, when mainstream media newsrooms themselves were
shifting towards more networked forms of journalism involving crowd-sourcing, blogging and public participation.[21] Just
like any mainstream mass media organization, WikiLeaks
clearly wanted a wide audience and to have an impact on
society. It did not see itself as a niche or personal project.
WikiLeaks' staff believed passionately that they were revealing hidden facts that the wider public needed to be aware of
and even act upon. All these are familiar elements of certain
kinds of traditional campaigning journalism. In this sense
the argument about whether WikiLeaks should be defined
as journalism is cyclical. Those who argue that WikiLeaks
is not 'journalism' are defining the term to exclude forms
of news mediation that they do not wish to give an official
stamp. Those who argue that WikiLeaks easily fits into
their definition of journalism are in danger of ignoring how
it challenges the validity of those categories. The debate
about 'WikiLeaks as Journalism' is really a debate about
what journalism is or is becoming. Instead of asking whether
WikiLeaks is journalism or not, we should ask 'What kind
of journalism is WikiLeaks creating?' The challenge to the
rest of journalism is to come up with something as good, if
not better.

## 1.2 THE CHALLENGE OF WIKILEAKS TO ALTERNATIVE JOURNALISM

WikiLeaks can be said to provide a challenge to much of
conventional journalism, but it also interrogates the idea
of so-called 'alternative media': the journalism that self-
consciously sets itself apart from the dominant ideology or
practice of mainstream news media. During its development
it experimented with many of the forms and means used

by the alternative media across the web. As well as its basic 'drop box' function, it used novel online practices such as Wikis, crowd-sourcing, forums, and email lists. Implicit in the use of these was a production philosophy that was participatory and open source. As it adapted, rejected and shifted from alternative, collaborative methods to its current hybrid status, it has created models but also highlighted many problems for those in the more experimental and less orthodox parts of the media landscape.

In this first phase of WikiLeaks between 2006 and 2009 we see how its organization and activities contrast with mainstream journalism. At this point it appears to fit into a classic definition of alternative media.[22] At its simplest, 'alternative' is a negative distinction that means doing journalism that the mainstream does not. It can be an alternative to mainstream in content, style, organization, production processes, distribution methods and its relationship with the public, but – perhaps above all – in its purpose or aims.

WikiLeaks is independent of commercial, corporate, government or lobby-group control or ownership. It is a non-membership, non-profit organization funded by donations, with no governance structure. In its earliest days, an 'advisory board' was constantly under discussion, with attempts made to recruit, but this was never expected to have any overall ultimate control over the collective. There is no mutual ownership or control so it seemed more like an anarchist cell than a co-operative collective. It had overt political aims, though no clear policy-related programme. Its central aim was to foment change. A quote from an email leaked by Cryptome read: 'We feel that per hour spent this provides the greatest positive impact on the world and ourselves that is within our means to achieve.'

However, it did not conform to the model of an NGO or public advocacy group. So while it was awarded prizes by

NGOs such as the UK branch of Amnesty International it did not want to be part of their world.[23] According to some accounts, there were a few important people who contributed to its evolution and management at this stage, but Julian Assange was, in effect, to become the dominant and controlling figure.

At this early stage WikiLeaks was also quite different from the online campaigning groups such as MoveOn in America, which are essentially digital activism platforms seeking to promote or widen political engagement. WikiLeaks was about information, not practical politics. WikiLeaks at this stage appeared to have more in common with initiatives like Cryptome, which was, as we have seen, actually connected to WikiLeaks in its earliest phase. This is a website which since 1996 has provided information – including leaked documents – about intelligence and security issues:

> Cryptome welcomes documents for publication that are prohibited by governments worldwide, in particular material on freedom of expression, privacy, cryptology, dual-use technologies, national security, intelligence, and secret governance – open, secret and classified documents – but not limited to those. Documents are removed from this site only by order served directly by a US court having jurisdiction. No court order has ever been served; any order served will be published here – or elsewhere if gagged by order. Bluffs will be published if comical but otherwise ignored.[24]

Cryptome differed markedly even at this point from WikiLeaks, as a much more ideologically coherent project. It is an avowedly niche anti-hegemonic site with an academic underpinning. As we have seen, the main author John Young became a strong critic of WikiLeaks, implying it had compromised by its associations with mainstream media and a failure to maintain a strict anti-capitalist agenda. Despite starting up in 1996, Cryptome has failed to achieve the impact or profile WikiLeaks managed to attain within its first few years. In that sense it was the kind of classic semi-underground, rigorously alternative media organization that Assange was keen for WikiLeaks not to become. He personally had much larger ambitions:

> We all only live once. So we are obligated to make good use of the time that we have and to do something that is meaningful and satisfying. This is something that I find meaningful and satisfying. That is my temperament. I enjoy creating systems on a grand scale, and I enjoy helping people who are vulnerable. And I enjoy crushing bastards. So it is enjoyable work.[25]

In what way was this ambition to 'crush bastards' consistent with a typology of alternative political media? Assange certainly wanted to be an alternative to mainstream media. He was critical of what he saw as its complicity in covering up injustice in authoritarian states as well as liberal democracies:[26] 'we in the West have deluded ourselves into believing that we actually have a truly free press. We don't. And we can see that in the difference between what WikiLeaks does and what the rest of the press does.'[27]

However, he was never particularly interested in creating an alternative audience. Indeed, early users were urged to share what they learned on WikiLeaks with local mainstream outlets to promulgate the news. This flew in the face of the typical route for much of the political blogosphere.

Some sites, such as liberal group blog 'The Daily Kos' in America, have achieved substantial scale. However, it is not an ideological challenge to either mainstream media or politics. It seeks to influence the mainstream agenda not to subvert it. In contrast, groups like the radical UK news aggregator Indymedia were prepared to sacrifice reach in favour of a more distinct positioning that satisfied a particular 'anti-globalization' audience. However, it has had almost no impact on wider public attitudes, nor has it managed to influence the mainstream political or media agenda. Assange realized that to effect immediate political change he needed to reach out to a mass audience that could mobilize public opinion to put pressure on those in power, especially given the naïve-anarchic view in WikiLeaks' earliest days that the publication of leaks alone would change history:

> you should remember Solzhenitsyn's words, that, 'In the right moment, one word of truth outweighs the world.' Solzhenitsyn was referring to a world of lies. But this still is true of free information across the world, and it's also true of the information in the West, that, in some cases, one classified video can possibly stop a war, and maybe fifty – definitely can.[28]

Assange showed no special desire to work with civil society organizations or political groups to achieve these aims. In WikiLeaks' earliest days, none of those were willing to fund the radical project. While happy to accept the kudos of an Index on Censorship award, he was unwilling to work with them until much later. While these organizations sought to have a progressive, reformist relationship with those in power, Assange wanted to disrupt the systems that sustained those in authority. Critically, he does not identify an ideological stance or a political issue in particular that he is opposing, but the role of knowledge in politics itself:

> What most people see is an illusion. Because what most people get is news that comes from press releases. Or it's

news that even comes from a human rights organization that is writing news in part to tell you something but also in part to keep its funding. And most information that comes to you is targeted at you. It is designed in some small way to manipulate you, so it is a deviation from the truth. But the internal documents of major corporations and intelligence agencies and governments are designed for their internal use. For some internal process that is occurring, some internal logistical structure. They're not designed to manipulate you. And because of that difference in perceived audience you can start to see how major organizations work, and it's not how people think they work – it's something different. And if we are to produce a more civilized society, a more just society, it has to be based upon the truth. Because judgements which are not based upon the truth can only lead to outcomes which are themselves false.[29]

So if WikiLeaks is a threat to power in this phase, it is as a force of disruption in the way authority mediates itself. It is an attempted assault upon the control of information as a precondition to political change, not a campaign to achieve a particular policy goal or to promote a political faction or movement.

In some ways, at this stage WikiLeaks appears to have some of the characteristics of 'rhizomatic' alternative media, a more protean form of anti-mainstream organization or network that is prepared to deal critically with both state and market, but that operates according to its own imperatives, principles and methods:

The approach to alternative media as rhizomatic also makes it possible to highlight the fluidity and contingency of (community) media organizations, in contrast to the more rigid ways mainstream public and commercial media often (have to) function. The elusive identity of alternative media means that they can – by their mere existence and functioning – question and destabilize the rigidities and certainties of public and commercial media organizations. At the same time, their elusiveness makes alternative media hard to control and to encapsulate in legislation, thus guaranteeing their independence.[30]

By its very nature, a 'rhizomatic' form of alternative media is not necessarily static. WikiLeaks embraces the uncertainty principle. By adopting different aspects of various media/political organizations, WikiLeaks appears in this phase to have created a hybridized, multi-faceted media entity combining elements of the following models:

- hacktavist network
- transparency organization
- political sect
- stateless group
- uncensorable outlet.

What was WikiLeaks an alternative to? At this point it's important to remind ourselves that mainstream media is also in flux. The definition of differences between mainstream and alternative were becoming blurred. Indeed, the definition of journalism itself was also being challenged. WikiLeaks is very much part of this process.

## 1.3 THE CHALLENGE OF WIKILEAKS TO MAINSTREAM MEDIA JOURNALISM

The same new digital communications environment that provided the conditions for WikiLeaks also created a period of unprecedented transformation for mainstream news media.

The Internet, digitization and related social and economic changes are turning old models of media production, dissemination and consumption upside-down.[31] This is a period of rapid and radical transition for journalism. It is moving from a closed to an open system. Deadlines are dissolving as news is personalized by consumers into an on-demand service. Where the infrastructure and resources allow, information is now endlessly available, interactive, connected and editable. The Internet now networks information that was previously compartmentalized into government, business, personal and public data and retained by those people or groups. There is no longer any need to wait for the news media to gather, filter and package information. Citizens and organizations can transmit and receive it themselves.

This means that the flow of information is now increasingly occurring outside of traditional mainstream news media. Previously, the news media were virtually the only public platform for accessing topical facts, comment, analysis and debate. Now much of that discourse has been disintermediated. As WikiLeaks itself has shown, cost barriers to creating an online media platform are so low as to be insignificant. Contrast that with the cost of investing in a printing plant, a TV studio or any kind of traditional professional mass media newsroom. All this means that mainstream journalism is facing two major threats. One is economic; the other is editorial competition. Of course, the two are related and both are relevant to the evolution of WikiLeaks. How journalism deals with those threats will also determine how it handles the deeper shifts in the role of information in politics and society.

Mainstream news media in the West is facing a business crisis as the Internet erodes its sources of revenue. News media elsewhere in the world may be growing sales and audiences as developing countries expand their media markets,

but the old business model will face similar structural challenges there, too. In most developed countries, newspaper
sales are declining over the long term, and while TV audiences are not plummeting, advertising is moving into other,
cheaper, online platforms. There is still huge value in many
of these legacy media organizations, especially as they adapt
and move online. They have strong brands, high profile and
reputations of affinity and trust with their audiences. They
also have editorial experience and resources that add to
their physical and legal assets. Some are experimenting with
new payment mechanisms that may provide a viable business model. However, free access to online news is making
it harder to monetize their web-based operations even where
they are able to attract attention and traffic. For example,
the *Guardian* website, guardian.co.uk, is the fifth-most-read
newspaper website in the world, with around 30 million
unique visits per month. Yet the paper *Guardian* newspaper
is only the ninth most-read paper in the UK. Even combined
they are bringing in much less revenue than that generated
by 400,000 readers for the dead-tree version in the past.[32]

This has led to severe pressure on editorial resources in
mainstream media. It is not enough simply to count heads,
but attempts to measure the decline in original production
do generally indicate increased constraints on the quality
of work.[33] Of course, digitization brings huge efficiencies
and productivity gains. You only have to consider the time-
savings brought by mobile phones and Internet research.
Then add on much faster editing technologies and the
benefits of free 'user-generated content'. The response of a
healthy innovative newsroom should be to make the most
of all these new tools and to adopt Jeff Jarvis' nostrum of
'cover what you do best and link to the rest'.[34] Traditional
journalism always spent much of its time recycling copy
and duplicating the work of other outlets. In a sense, the

Internet has merely exposed the inefficiency of traditional, linear media as a delivery mechanism for information and deliberation. Now every act of journalism must add value. This means seeking more genuinely original and useful or attractive material and/or quicker and better ways to connect people to it. Even then, it is clear that the Golden Age of massive newsrooms funded by pseudo-monopoly advertising revenues is over. Too many commercial media organizations have asset-stripped declining businesses instead of building on new technologies and diversifying into related communications services. So, especially in this transition phase, there was no growth in quality mass mainstream journalism outside of elite media, and arguably a decline – especially in the areas of challenging, controversial, risky political and investigative journalism in mass media outlets.

This economic threat is exacerbated by the editorial challenge of online competitors. New online news sources are emerging that offer information directly to the public for free, anytime they want it. Most important are aggregating sites that can recycle material for nothing. Search itself means that people can access individual bits of information in isolation. Google News and Google Search do not employ many journalists but they are now hugely significant sources for news.[35] Social networks also recycle material that is linked to or cut and pasted onto platforms like Twitter or Facebook. It means that any information in the public domain is now instantly disseminated through hyperlinks. A new fact put online immediately loses any exclusivity. The state of information as well as analysis and comment has moved from being scarce to super-abundant.

On top of this there are now a whole range of non-mainstream-media producers of journalism. The so-called blogosphere has now attained such a scale and diversity that the term is almost meaningless. As well as the classic individual bloggers there are now substantial group blogs that cover every topic that mainstream media ever considered and much more. Virtually every public government department, business and civil society organization now has a website, often with a blog element. Everyone from the US State Department to the British monarchy is now on Twitter and Facebook, often connected to slick websites with video, audio and comment pages. They can now communicate directly with the public in a two-way conversation that can cut out the traditional journalistic intermediary.

This has also created opportunities for new forms of mainstream journalism. Some, like the Huffington Post, are hybrids of the new independent producers and the mainstream media models. So Arianna Huffington's (largely) political website has some paid full-time staff but mainly depends on unpaid writers and the aggregation of other publications' content. It makes money and has been sold to AOL. Another example is Mumsnet in the UK. This has a tiny paid staff who help edit the parenting website that provides news about products, services and developments in family matters. But its main attraction is provided by a series of hugely popular forums. These are lightly moderated but the content is largely driven by the site members. The website has become such an important forum for its demographic that all British political leaders now court its readers by giving online interviews to Mumsnet's members in the same way that they appear on mainstream TV chat-shows.

There has been a wholesale shift of Western mainstream mass media to a networked journalism model. Virtually all legacy media organizations have now changed the way they gather and disseminate news to reflect the realities described above. This has been a relatively recent move. When Charlie Beckett described networked journalism in *SuperMedia* (published 2008) it was still an aspiration or innovation. Public participation in mainstream journalism was widely conceived as a threat that could be countered or ignored – even outlawed. By 2010 when Polis, the media think-tank at the London School of Economics, published a report on the state of networked journalism in the UK, it had become a widespread reality, albeit still seen in many media companies as additional to rather than replacing traditional practice.[36] Globally, we see that the first great phase of adoption and adaption of networked journalism is in full swing and that the trends indicate that its effects will deepen and extend. The rapid development of new technological platforms such as Internet-enabled mobile phones and tablet devices with greater interactivity and personalization, combined with the development of more social networking platforms, means that the networked nature of news production can only increase.

At one level, networked journalism is a practical matter of how journalists acquire information. It means gathering user-generated content directly from the public or from other online sources. This is why TV news bulletins now routinely include 'amateur' footage. It is why witnesses on Twitter or Facebook are regularly quoted in news stories. Imagery is now sourced by networked journalists from the vast amounts of pictures uploaded by the public to Flickr, Twitpic or yfrog. But it can go beyond this, for example, to harvesting the wisdom in the crowds. Journalists can appeal for information or for expertise or simply survey what the public thinks about an issue or event. The public is also much more intimately part of the conversation around an event. Instead of lofty columnists handing down opinions, there is a lively and often rude exchange of views through online comment and forums. This reaches its formal apogee in the 'live blog' where a journalist or news team covers a single event or issue with a continuous, multi-dimensional online web-page story. As it updates it links and recycles other sources – video clips, Tweets, agency information, official statements, reader emails and anything else that can add detail, context or drama to the narrative. It is the journalist as a facilitator of an information flow rather than the main witness or author of a final version of reality. Within five years it has moved from a novelty seen fit only for sports events and culture blogs to a staple of news coverage for the newspapers and broadcasters, like the *Guardian*, the BBC and beyond. National Public Radio's Andy Carvin even does it as a Twitter feed.

We shall see in chapter 2 how this increased 'networkedness' creates ethical and editorial issues for journalism as ideas of objectivity and transparency are strained to breaking point – especially when it means connecting to journalistic organizations with different ideologies or cultures. But it was into this already turbulent reshaping of journalism that WikiLeaks emerged.

One of the first such cases was that of oil giant Trafigura. In 2009, reporters for the *Guardian* newspaper and the flagship BBC current affairs programme *Newsnight* obtained a damning report on a 2006 incident centred around the dumping of toxic waste off the Ivory Coast. Alongside an MP, Paul Farrelly, the teams attempted to publish their stories despite Trafigura's best attempts to obtain a legal injunction barring them from doing so.

As part of such efforts, Farrelly put down a Parliamentary Question relating to the report. The proceedings of the UK's parliament are regarded as protected speech in the UK. MPs have the unqualified privilege to say anything in parliament. Journalists have qualified privilege to report what MPs say. However, in this instance, a judge ruled against lifting the injunction and the reporting ban remained. Furthermore, the reporters were banned from revealing Trafigura had obtained such an order. The result was one of the earliest revelations of the incendiary effects when social and mainstream media mix.

A delicately worded and nigh-on incomprehensible article, neither naming the company involved nor publishing documents, appeared on the front page of the *Guardian* on 12 October 2009, under the byline of the newspaper's experienced investigations editor David Leigh. Within minutes, thousands of Twitter users in the UK and beyond had deciphered the article using information available elsewhere on the Internet and named Trafigura.

Someone, too, had involved WikiLeaks. It is not clear whether it was an activist inspired by previous reporting, another associate or whistle-blower, or even – according to some theories – one of the reporters themselves. The full, injuncted report appeared on WikiLeaks, and was linked to by thousands of users, breaking the court order. Within hours, the High Court reversed its stance, and the full story could finally be told by the UK media. The story may not have been WikiLeaks' through-and-through like so many later revelations, but the incident brought to light how WikiLeaks and the wider networks it inhabits are often at their strongest where conventional journalists are weak.

The Trafigura episode characterizes exactly how the Internet is challenging the role of mainstream media in the mediation of power. The case showed that the balance between information privacy or property and the public interest was being shifted by the affordances of the new technologies. The practical limits on journalism were being expanded exponentially. Along with that, as we shall see in chapter 3, the way that traditional mass media framed narratives and the issues that they chose to put on the agenda were also being questioned.

## 1.4 THE CHALLENGE OF WIKILEAKS TO POWER

WikiLeaks was always conceived as a disruptive political project. As we have seen, Julian Assange was explicit in his desire to attack the networks of information secrecy that sustained the networks of power. It is worth looking at length at this extract from Assange's 2006 essay.[37] This is how he describes the structure of power as the communicative relationship between 'conspirators':

> First take some nails ('conspirators') and hammer them into a board at random. Then take twine ('communication') and loop it from nail to nail without breaking. Call the twine connecting two nails a link. Unbroken twine means it is possible to travel from any nail to any other nail via twine and intermediary nails. Mathematicians say that this type of graph is connected.
>
> Information flows from conspirator to conspirator. Not every conspirator trusts or knows every other conspirator even though all are connected. Some are on the fringe of the conspiracy, others are central and communicate with many conspirators and others still may know only two conspirators but be a bridge between important sections or groupings of the conspiracy.

To challenge power you must intervene in this 'conspiracy': 'We can deceive or blind a conspiracy by distorting or restricting the information available to it. We can reduce total conspiratorial power via unstructured attacks on links or through throttling and separating. A conspiracy sufficiently engaged in this manner is no longer able to comprehend its environment and plan robust action.'[38]

With this striking metaphor Assange is sketching out a

theory of how WikiLeaks can become a 'Network Exploit', an intervention in a system that takes advantage of its structure and even strengths to resist its power.[39] What better way to make manifest the conspiracy than by literally making it visible? WikiLeaks' single most famous leak in this early phase did exactly that. On 5 April 2010, the site released a heavily edited 17-minute video from the cockpit of a US army Apache helicopter in Iraq.[40]

The edited film opened with a graphicized quote from George Orwell: 'Political language is designed to make lies sound truthful and murder respectable, and to give the appearance of solidity to pure wind.'

The footage is a compelling narrative of a military operation that gives the viewer the American combatants' perspective. It contains shocking scenes. A group of armed Iraqis, plus two Reuters employees speaking with them, are shot and killed – though at the time the pilots are unaware that any of them are journalists. An Iraqi father taking his children to school stops to assist one of the wounded journalists in the aftermath. He too is shot and killed. His children, who remained in the heavily damaged car, were wounded but survived. WikiLeaks journalist Kristinn Hrafnsson, who travelled to Iraq with cameraman Ingi Ingasson to meet survivors featured in the footage, says it was for that death of an innocent civilian that the video was named 'Collateral Murder' – not for the deaths of the journalists. Perhaps most shocking of all was the callous attitude shown by the crew of the Apache helicopter. 'Oh yeah, look at those dead bastards', one is heard to say to his co-pilot.

WikiLeaks had worked for weeks in Iceland to edit and release the video. Despite promoting the shortened, heavily edited version of the video, WikiLeaks stayed true to its principles of releasing source material, and also issued the full, unedited, 39-minute-long video. This also featured the same helicopter, call sign 'Crazyhorse one-eight', in another incident, firing a Hellfire missile into a building, despite a bystander walking past at the moment of launch.

The decision to editorialize was a controversial one. The short version of the footage omitted a scene showing one of the men shot had apparently been carrying an RPG (rocket-propelled grenade). Assange's statements in interviews that the edited version was produced to create 'maximum political impact'[41] were used as a evidence of editorializing. Even the name 'Collateral Murder' was questioned, given that some of those killed seemed to be members of the armed struggle against the American occupation.

Assange felt that the video achieved precisely its objective of challenging the ability of the powerful to dictate a 'false' narrative:

> This video shows what modern warfare has become, and, I think, after seeing it, whenever people hear about a certain number of casualties that resulted during fighting with close air support, they will understand what is going on ... The video also makes clear that civilians are listed as insurgents automatically, unless they are children, and that bystanders who are killed are not even mentioned.[42]

The video was also the first to prompt a reaction to WikiLeaks from senior figures within the American administration. Defense Secretary Robert Gates condemned the video for failing to show the hostile context in which US soldiers were operating: 'They're in a combat situation. The video doesn't show the broader picture of the firing that was going on at American troops. It's obviously a hard thing to see. It's painful to see, especially when you learn after the fact what was going on. But these people were operating in split second situations.'[43]

The wider response of the US government was muted. Asked about the footage in his 7 April 2010 briefing, White House Press Secretary Robert Gibbs neglected to condemn the leak of the footage, instead agreeing it was 'very graphic in nature and extremely tragic' and stressing the tough climate in which the US army was operating.[44]

In a remark which in hindsight was laced with irony, Defense Secretary Robert Gates complained the Collateral Murder video was like looking at the conflict 'through a soda straw' – a picture far too narrow to draw out meaningful conclusions, and easily subject to distortion. What WikiLeaks did next, if anything, granted Gates his wish – and provoked a far more aggressive response from the Obama administration.

Collateral Murder was more than just the first of the leaks believed to have been received from Bradley Manning. Unlike the larger document dumps – which WikiLeaks possessed by the time of the video's publication – it was small enough for WikiLeaks to edit and produce with its own resources. Even more than the subsequent releases, the video heralded WikiLeaks' shift from a wiki-style home for documents to a more complex hybrid.

WikiLeaks had to use almost all of its resources to do so, however. Assange, some of his techs, and leading supporters such as Icelandic MP Birgitta Jonsdottir all gathered together and worked day after day on the release – in addition to the trip to Iraq by two WikiLeakers. This stalled all other everyday operations by the site. This was the beginning of tensions between Julian and other supporters which would reach a head in the following months. WikiLeaks' internal and external transformations were accelerating apace.

Also present in what was informally dubbed the 'bunker' for several days, was journalist Raffi Khatchadourian, whose *New Yorker* profile includes a succinct summary of where

Julian Assange's philosophy for the site had shifted to by this point:

> I want to set up a new standard: 'scientific journalism'. If you publish a paper on DNA, you are required, by all the good biological journals, to submit the data that has informed your research – the idea being that people will replicate it, check it, verify it. So this is something that needs to be done for journalism as well. There is an immediate power imbalance, in that readers are unable to verify what they are being told, and that leads to abuse.[45]

In effect, because WikiLeaks publishes its source material, Assange believes that it is free to offer its analysis, no matter how speculative. Indeed, WikiLeaks had submitted its own analysis and interpretations of its material since the start. Shifting to editing the material, or selecting its key features, was a minor transition from this point. What distinguished – and still distinguishes – WikiLeaks from the mainstream is its insistence on publishing full source material alongside its interpretation of the facts.

At this point we can see that WikiLeaks is pushing at the boundaries of the typology of an alternative media organization. It is certainly a threat to the status quo – both media and political. That is why it began to come under sustained attack from both press and politicians. In response to that, it began pursuing the Iceland Media Initiative with Icelandic MP Birgitta Jonsdottir. This was an attempt to turn Iceland into a free media haven, a constitutionally guarded space where organizations like WikiLeaks would be safe from legal assault.[46] At this point WikiLeaks was certainly conforming to the idea of independent watchdog media, holding authority to account by giving evidence for abuses of power. For all its distortions and rhetorical flourishes, the Collateral Murder project did give strong evidence that the American military was not being entirely honest in its disclosures about civilian deaths. By continuing to protect its sources WikiLeaks was exposing the limits of the authorities' powers (or at least those in democratic states) to prevent exposure. The fact that it had a different risk calculation from conventional media meant that it was much more relaxed about putting this kind of material into the public domain. As we shall see in chapter 2, that was not without ethical problems.* But this was not enough. What seemed to surprise WikiLeaks was the relative lack of interest from the wider media and general public in this exposé of one graphic incident. To Assange and his team it seemed logical to try to find bigger stories and a way of disseminating them that would have the kind of impact on those in power that was the ultimate objective of WikiLeaks itself.

---

* See the Epilogue for a summary of the latest and highly significant developments on these issues at the end of August 2011 when WikiLeaks released all the Embassy cables in full.

# 2

# THE GREATEST STORY EVER TOLD?
# THE AFGHAN WAR LOGS, IRAQ WAR
# LOGS AND THE EMBASSY CABLES

## 2.1 INTRODUCTION

In 2010 WikiLeaks achieved its biggest ever publication of classified information, bringing it into direct confrontation with the most powerful nation on earth. It reached a vast global audience directly and Julian Assange and WikiLeaks became one of the best-known and most talked about media brands in the world. To do this, it became extensively networked into mainstream media across the globe. It transformed itself from an independent whistle-blower publisher that made occasional deals with traditional journalists, into one working almost continually with other news organizations in relatively formal, albeit sometimes unstable, relationships. The operational model had been reinvented. Now contracts were signed and working agreements made, and resources were shared. It was primarily in a collective deal with the *Guardian* and *New York Times*, *Der Spiegel* and *El País* – but subsequently also with a range of other mainstream media internationally through individual ad hoc arrangements. The WikiLeaks franchise was rolled out across the world.

The Afghan war logs were followed within six months by the Iraq war logs and the American Embassy cable releases. It was the largest unauthorized publication of confidential government information in the history of modern journalism. WikiLeaks was effectively selling its leaks wholesale to news retailers, although Julian Assange and his team remained intimately involved in the act of dissemination. Accounts of the negotiations that took place between Assange and the professional mainstream media journalists reveal that the arrangements developed over the period of the partnerships and were sometimes fractious. This was more than a personality clash, although it is clear that emotions and egos on both sides were not always kept under control. More seriously, there was a mismatch of principles, practice and purpose. Yet it was also an astoundingly successful series of acts of journalism that continued beyond 2010.

This new strategy attempted to combine WikiLeaks' core idea of disruptive alternative journalism based on a largely unmediated release of data with the evolving practice of mainstream networked journalism. In themselves these data releases took the concept of revelation far beyond the classic journalistic idea of a scoop: a specific piece of information that can shed light on a wider hidden truth. In the case of the Afghan, Iraq and cables leaks, the public was given a comprehensive, detailed and extensive amount of data – although it is completely wrong to make the mistake of many critics in calling it a 'data dump'. Only a proportion of the material was released and almost always with a significant degree of editorial oversight. Assange himself made the comparison[1] with the 1971 'Pentagon Papers' episode in which Daniel Ellsberg copied and leaked 7,000 papers from a classified

report on the conduct of the Vietnam War. Only a few hundred were used in the first *New York Times* reports.[2] A book
with fuller details of thousands of the documents was only
published five years later. With the WikiLeaks revelations,
far more information was put online straight away. The
Internet meant the global public was also able to contribute
to analysing and contextualizing that data immediately, too.
WikiLeaks was not able to do this all on its own. It combined with various mainstream news organizations. It did so
mainly to access a much wider audience but also because its
partners could provide help in processing the information.
This strained but ultimately fruitful relationship highlighted
some of the tensions and even contradictions inherent in
WikiLeaks as well as the limits on mainstream media that we
will explore here in chapter 2.*

## 2.2 COLLABORATION AND THE AFGHAN WAR LOGS

WikiLeaks' release of the Collateral Murder video in April
2010 had brought the site to the attention of the world's
media on a scale dozens of times larger than any of its previous releases. For the first time, mainstream media outlets
began to run stories speculating about WikiLeaks' next
release. The consensus view was that more videos were
imminent: footage of a 2009 US airstrike in Afghanistan that
killed dozens of civilians was the most confidently expected.[3]
    What the media did not notice was a single, undistin-
guished leak which occurred six days before the release of
the Collateral Murder video: a single diplomatic cable origi-

---

* See the Epilogue for a summary of the latest and highly significant
developments on these issues at the end of August 2011 when WikiLeaks
released all the Embassy cables in full.

nating from Iceland. It served as WikiLeaks' way of verifying an unbelievable cache of documents: 91,000 military records from Afghanistan; 391,000 records from Iraq; and more than 250,000 confidential diplomatic dispatches. Each in its own right would be the largest leak of classified material in history. Collectively, they formed an almost unimaginably large security breach.

The circumstances which led to such huge volumes of materials coming into WikiLeaks' hands are themselves extraordinary. In the fallout of the September 2001 attacks on America and the intelligence shortcomings which hindered efforts to prevent them, the American government vastly widened access to much of its classified military material through a network known as SIPRNET. Poor understanding of the system by many officials meant substantial quantities of material with no military connection also ended up on the system. Up to 3 million military and civilian employees, and external contractors, had access to some quantity of classified material through the network.

One individual with access to SIPRNET was the gifted but troubled Private First Class Bradley Manning, the man alleged to have passed the intelligence material to WikiLeaks. Stationed at a base in Iraq, Manning is alleged to have worked out how to expand his legitimate access to the system to allow him to download large numbers of cables and field documents in batches. The computers used for access were cut off from the Internet and USB keys, but no one thought to prevent transferring information, or 'writing', to CD.

According to chat logs, or records of online 'conversations' given to *Wired* magazine by Adrian Lamo, the ex-hacker who eventually turned Manning over to the authorities, Manning took in CDs containing Lady Gaga's music.[4] Feigning singing along to the tracks, Manning wiped the CDs of their musical content and replaced it with the classified materials. All this took place just weeks before WikiLeaks published its test cable: all three batches of data extend to 28 February 2010.

The least-known aspect of the leak is how the material left Bradley Manning's hands and fell into those belonging to WikiLeaks. Through an ex-boyfriend, Manning came to know many close to the hacking community at the Massachusetts Institute of Technology, some of whom had links to WikiLeaks. This community is now a subject of the Grand Jury investigation into WikiLeaks and Manning.

WikiLeaks had obtained material that virtually any news outlet in the world would want. It now had to decide what to do with it. The scale of the task for an outlet with no formal structures and fewer than ten people working even close to full-time was unbelievable: to verify, filter through and find stories in hundreds of millions of words of material – not to mention to decide whether to redact the material or publish in full. The problems were heightened by mounting internal divisions within WikiLeaks over whether the material was too much, too fast for the whistle-blowing site. Tensions grew between Daniel Domscheit-Berg, and others, and Julian Assange over WikiLeaks' growing focus on the US. There was also disagreement with the idea of all but closing down the site's other operations and stream of smaller leaks to focus on a few big-ticket items. Assange and others had grown disillusioned with the site's original intention to simply publish material in the hope Internet users would sift through it for stories. They wanted more high-profile results and a more direct way of achieving them.

WikiLeaks had more material than it could cope with, and could not agree internally on the best way to move forwards – other than to fulfil its stated aim to maximize its impact. This was the climate Nick Davies, a veteran investigative reporter at the *Guardian*, walked into when he met Julian Assange in a Belgian café. Davies had seen Assange in interviews and other broadcasts talking about his site and future releases, and decided to offer up his services – and possibly those of the *Guardian* – for a much greater level of cooperation on future releases. Working through a small number of mutual contacts in the UK, Davies managed to get word of an event Assange would be attending, and secured a chat.

Despite the apparent contradictions – Davies an old-school reporter for the mainstream media, Assange an ex-hacker at the front of the online transparency movement – the two had much in common. Assange called for 'scientific journalism' through the publication of source material. Davies, through his book *Flat Earth News*[5] called on mainstream media to raise its game and report more accurately and courageously. The meeting went well. Within hours Davies had secured a preliminary agreement granting the *Guardian* advance access to WikiLeaks' next major release: the Afghan war logs. Details of a server and password through which the material could soon be accessed were sketched onto a napkin. Davies secured the agreement of Alan Rusbridger, the paper's editor, to devote resources to work on the story, and the project was underway.

It quickly became apparent that the mainstream media had constraints WikiLeaks had previously been free from. The legal status of the material was initially unknown: was it in breach of the UK's Official Secrets Act? How would the government react – would they censor publication? WikiLeaks might transcend national boundaries, but mainstream news organizations do not. To solve this problem, a virtually unprecedented collaboration was proposed, and agreed: international news organizations would come onboard. Taking advantage of the close relationship between the *Guardian* and the *New York Times*, and indeed between editors Alan Rusbridger and Bill Keller, the US media giant was brought onboard. Given that the *Times* itself could also face censorship, because the material was of US military origin, German periodical *Der Spiegel* was also included in the coalition.

Both the *Guardian* and WikiLeaks claim the credit for the eventual team working on the Afghan records – though it seems most likely that, with its pre-existing relationships, it was the newspaper rather than Assange that brought everyone together. The outlets and WikiLeaks agreed on a starting date, and occasionally, informally, shared the top lines of their stories, but they did not collaborate on material or agree on the editorial direction taken, on particular stories or overall.

This first collaboration also highlighted some of the short-comings of mainstream media in handling the sheer volume of data concerned. Reporters working from the *Guardian*'s sparkling brand new offices in King's Place, London, were accessing the Afghan database through Microsoft Excel – using the spreadsheet software to search through 66,000 records. The problem was, the Afghan data contained 91,000 records. By using an old version of the software, reporters had accidentally cut off almost a third of the records. The mistake persisted for a few days before it was spotted, apparently by Julian Assange himself.

Other issues were less clear-cut. Reporters browsing the military records soon saw thousands of the documents contained details on informants: names, what information had been passed over, phone numbers and even GPS coordinates. Several became concerned that, were WikiLeaks to publish the Afghan war logs in full, those informants' lives could be put in jeopardy. However, neither WikiLeaks nor the mainstream news organizations possessed the resources to redact 91,000 documents manually for harm minimization – and while the newspapers might have been willing to go without publishing source material, WikiLeaks emphatically was not. The eventual messy compromise satisfied no-one. Reporters identified the 15,000 documents categorized as 'threat reports' as the ones most likely to contain sensitive information in need of redaction. WikiLeaks agreed to hold these documents back while publishing the remainder in full. But when the stories and war logs were eventually made public, it quickly emerged that many of the other categories also contained details on informants. It should be noted, however, that as at June 2011, the US State Department acknowledged it had no evidence of direct harm to any individuals as a result of the publication of the leak.[6]

WikiLeaks eventually quietly published the remaining cables with redactions late in 2010. It had attempted to crowd-source the redaction process, with little success due to lack of user interest and problems with trust: how could the site verify potential users were fit to view unredacted material? Eventually, a Norwegian newspaper agreed to verify the documents in exchange for belated access.

Back in the weeks ahead of the release of the Afghan war logs, the second major point of tension between WikiLeaks and its mainstream partners raised its head: right to reply. Most mainstream journalists accept the principle that those targeted by a story should have the opportunity to respond on the veracity of claims made, and also (to an extent) to set out their version of events and response to a story.

For the war logs, this was not without risks. The unique publishing collaboration had been set up to make attempting to block publication by the mainstream media difficult, if not impossible. It meant it would require three jurisdictions to act identically and simultaneously. Even then, WikiLeaks as a publishing fallback made censorship unlikely, if not impossible. However, notifying the US Department of Defense as to what was to come could have resulted in censorship, leaks, condemnation and possibly even legal action. Nonetheless, the mainstream outlets agreed this was the right thing to do and coordinated their contact through the *New York Times*.

However, there was no clear new media / old media dichotomy on right to reply. The *New York Times* gave the Department of Defense sight of all of the war logs documents it intended to publish, as well as overall details on the scope of the leak. The other publications, while agreeing on the overall wisdom of approaching the Department of Defense, were unwilling to share full lists of all documents they were planning to publish. WikiLeaks represented one end on a spectrum of views across traditional media, rather than a totally alien approach.

The Afghan war logs were published on 25 July 2010, simultaneously across all outlets. Reaction from the US military was fierce. Defense Secretary Robert Gates said WikiLeaks was 'morally guilty' for putting lives at risk as a result of the leak, a view echoed by the chair of the Joint Chiefs of Staff. However, at this point Gates stressed US policies on access to information would not change: 'If one or a few members of the military did this, the notion that we would handicap our soldiers on the frontline by denying them this information . . . my bias is against that. I want those kids out there to have all the information they can have.'[7]

The Afghan documents had impact on the news agenda, and WikiLeaks and its partners were already at work on the next release, the same field combat reports covering five years of the war in Iraq. However, behind the scenes, key relationships were rapidly fraying.

## 2.3 THE IRAQ WAR LOGS – COLLABORATION UNDER STRESS

Nick Davies and Julian Assange were no longer speaking. Assange had contacted Stephen Grey, the author of *Ghost Plane*[8] and one of the key journalists behind uncovering extraordinary rendition. Without the knowledge of Davies or the mainstream media partners, Assange gave Grey access to the Afghan war documents, in order for the latter to work with the UK's *Channel 4 News*, a serious nightly one-hour news show produced by ITN, with a strong track record in investigative journalism. Assange told Grey[9] to contact Davies to arrange coordination and timing between outlets. Grey's call was the first idea Davies had that any other news organization had been added to the partnership. Assange defended the decision to pass on the information by saying the agreement between WikiLeaks and the *Guardian* covered print media only. The breach of trust proved fatal to the relationship between the two.

At the same time, WikiLeaks' internal divisions came to a head as Daniel Domscheit-Berg walked out after rejecting a 'suspension pending disciplinary hearing' issued by Assange. Several developers and volunteers walked out alongside him, leaving Assange with few core staff apart from some recent new hires picked up through the UK's Centre for Investigative Journalism. CIJ director Gavin MacFadyen was a core WikiLeaks supporter who had offered the services of interns, facilities, and even on occasion his sofa to the team.

WikiLeaks and its media coalition were now handling a database five times larger than the Afghan files, documenting a far bloodier and more political conflict – with strained relations and WikiLeaks in internal turmoil. It was at this point that Assange changed the terms of the deal again, seeking still-greater impact for his trove of material. Assange had decided to bring in a television team from the start for the Iraq war logs, to allow for a full documentary presentation of the material.

Thanks in large part to the urgings of Gavin MacFadyen, who set up initial meetings between Assange and editor Iain Overton, WikiLeaks chose a new not-for-profit journalism NGO named the Bureau of Investigative Journalism as its TV production house. At 1 a.m. on a Sunday morning in early August, Assange handed the Iraq files to the Bureau after a four-hour dinner, also attended by Al Jazeera – at which one of this book's co-authors was present.

The Bureau, at WikiLeaks' request, organized a hugely complex and ambitious series of commissions. It would produce a one-hour programme for Channel 4's *Dispatches*, including dispatching a crew to Iraq to meet people named in the documents, alongside one hour of English-language programming for Al Jazeera, plus an hour for Al Jazeera Arabic. The Bureau also produced a stand-alone website, iraqwarlogs.com, and hosted and cooperated with Swedish broadcaster SVT, which had independently been given the Iraq documents by Assange, and NGO Iraq Body Count, who had maintained one of the most authoritative death tallies in the seven years since the conflict began. When, one week before publication, Assange decided to add French newspaper *Le Monde* to the burgeoning group of collaborators, the Bureau also agreed to provide content there.

Just as WikiLeaks' resources were at their most stretched, what had already been an unprecedented collaboration of rival news organizations was made even more complex. It was at this point that the sex allegations against Julian Assange were made. Assange, while in Sweden, had stayed at the houses of two women, and had consensual sex with both. However, both claimed he had also had non-consensual sex by refusing to use a condom. Efforts by prosecutors to question Assange did not succeed, leading to an arrest warrant being issued. The presence of an arrest warrant made Assange unwilling to return to the country, leading to the eventual issuance of a European Arrest Warrant and the initiation of extradition proceedings. WikiLeaks' already overstretched operation was now spread even more thinly.

Assange's mainstream media partners were learning the difficulties of trying to manage such a complex network of news outlets. Each of the partners, in turn, were often also dealing directly with the source of the stories, Julian Assange himself. This was made harder for them as WikiLeaks seemed willing to change the deal with little or no notice. Due to the lengthy lead times for television, and the need to get a crew to Iraq, the timescale agreed by WikiLeaks and the print outlets was unmanageable for the Bureau of Investigative Journalism. At least four additional weeks were needed – taking the intended publication date from September to October. However, as WikiLeaks had already handed over the material to the print media partners, it had little ability to force a delay.

David Leigh, the *Guardian*'s investigations editor, had at this point taken on the mantle of doing the bulk of the day-to-day negotiations with WikiLeaks for the print media partners. He conceded a delay of the planned 'go' date with Assange, but at a price: WikiLeaks had to hand over its last remaining document tranche: the Embassy cables. Assange did so, on the condition that the *Guardian* agreed that the cables were stored for safekeeping and could not be published without Assange's agreement. WikiLeaks' control of the material was already starting to slip – a herald of things soon to come on a far grander scale.

Redaction was an even more problematic issue for the Iraq war logs than for their Afghan counterparts. It was a concern made all the more real as the inadequacies of the first redaction efforts had come to light. In addition to the previous concerns about minimizing harm to individuals on the ground, it was also known that redaction and potential harm would be the likeliest source of counter-attack from the White House and Department of Defense. All the mainstream outlets were agreed that redaction was essential. However, once again, none could shoulder the burden of combing through 391,000 documents totalling over 37 million words. This time no simple cutting of categories would suffice.

After protracted and heated debate, Assange conceded the need to redact the documents – more for strategic than for humanitarian reasons. The problem was now to work out how. It was a peculiar mix of old-media insistence on source protection and harm minimization, coupled with sophisticated networked techniques that produced the eventual solution.

It was coders working for Iraq Body Count (IBC) who hit upon a method. By using open-source online dictionaries, they could produce a script which would automatically black out any word not listed. WikiLeaks could decide the sensitivity of the redaction process, and IBC would code it. Journalists, particularly those at the Bureau of Investigative Journalism, contributed largely by breaking the system. Each time the redaction was declared 'finished', time would be spent looking for gaps. This led to the removal of professions from the data – as these could sometimes point to individuals – which again required the use of new open-source libraries. At other points, the word-length of redacted terms could be incriminating, so all redacted terms were made a standard duration. By a mix of high technology, open-source libraries, and low journalistic cunning, a system for eliminating all identifying information from the logs was produced. When the documents were published, journalists and the Department of Defense alike failed to find a single individual identified.

The downside was that the process rendered the documents almost unreadable. For the few hundred war logs each outlet was publishing to support its journalism, every one had to be manually redacted to ensure it remained comprehensible. Anyone hoping to search the logs on location would be thwarted. As the field reports were standardized documents, the redaction process didn't entirely obliterate their usefulness – but it became clear that trying to repeat the process for the far bigger Embassy cables leak to come would be impossible. WikiLeaks had more hurdles to jump – and was about to make its own task much harder.

## 2.4 THE CABLES AND THE LEGAL ATTACK

WikiLeaks and its partners had managed a far more complex coalition of organizations for the Iraq material than they did for the Afghanistan tranche, and despite growing fractiousness between some of the players, all had stuck to the agreed timetable. However, at the same time, events in Iceland were conspiring to ensure such an arrangement would be more difficult in future.

Transparency campaigner Heather Brooke, an expert on the UK's freedom of information laws and one of the driving forces behind an investigation into parliamentarians' expenses which saw dozens of MPs stand down, was researching her next book, on WikiLeaks and online secrecy. This had taken her to Iceland, where she met ex-WikiLeaker Smari McCarthy. He was eventually persuaded to hand her the full Embassy cables material for research purposes. For the first time, WikiLeaks had now suffered a major, uncontrolled, loss of material. The leaker had been leaked.

Fortunately for WikiLeaks and its media partners, Brooke took her material to the *Guardian*, where investigations editor David Leigh was able to bring her onto the paper's team working on the cables. But as a *Vanity Fair* profile of relations at the time attests, the incident shook Leigh's confidence in WikiLeaks' ability to keep hold of the material prior to publication. This led him to push for a much earlier 'go date' on the cables material than Assange intended. The *New York Times* and *Der Spiegel* concurred. The result was a showdown between Julian Assange, *Guardian* editor Alan Rusbridger, and the other parties:

> The three news organizations were poised to publish the material on November 8 . . . That was when Assange stormed into Rusbridger's office, threatening to sue. Rusbridger, Leigh, and the editors from *Der Spiegel* spent a marathon session with Assange, his lawyer, and [Kristinn] Hrafnsson, eventually restoring an uneasy calm. Some in the *Guardian* camp had wanted to break off relations with Assange entirely. Rusbridger somehow kept all parties at the table – a process involving a great deal of coffee followed by a great deal of wine. Ultimately he agreed to a further delay, allowing Assange time to bring in other media partners, this time France's *Le Monde* and Spain's *El País*.[10]

Assange had bought himself a month, and added two newspapers to the coalition. However, he intended to do much more. He was negotiating with Vaughan Smith, an ex-soldier and ex-journalist who had founded the Frontline Club, a private restaurant and meeting place for media professionals in Paddington, London. He struck a deal to use Smith's stately home in remote rural Norfolk as a base for WikiLeaks to house up to fifteen to twenty journalists to work directly on the Embassy cables. Assange planned to have the reporters – working largely on a voluntary basis – produce content based on the cables to be published directly on the WikiLeaks site, as well as published on a freelance basis by other papers across the world.

This added a huge extra burden to an already stressed organization. At this point, Assange was trying to keep his whereabouts unknown to avoid media interest in his ongoing Swedish sex trial. He needed to build the infrastructure for at least five distinct media organizations to publish and redact cables without duplication, as well as agreeing publishing schedules and more. No site had been built to host the cables. Now WikiLeaks also needed to fly journalists from around the world to Norfolk, provide them with cables and ways to search through them, and then to manage their copy.

WikiLeaks flew people in from South America, Russia, Australia, New Zealand and elsewhere, many of whom based themselves for days on campbeds in Smith's manor house. For some, the temptation was too much. Once they had cables, a few were reluctant to produce any content for WikiLeaks itself and quickly returned home to sell the material – or stories based on it – to papers in their own country. The others began preparing articles for the WikiLeaks site.

WikiLeaks had various motives for its approach. One was 'defensive': to avoid the backlash seen after previous releases. Assange wanted mechanisms to share material with rival papers in the UK and US markets to encourage them to moderate any criticism from the rest of the media and the establishment. The next was 'strategic': aimed at publishing cables to cement WikiLeaks' position in countries central to its interests, such as Sweden and Iceland. The third motive was 'opportunistic', aimed at expanding WikiLeaks' base and popularity in countries such as Brazil and Japan.

The move led to further deterioration of relations between WikiLeaks and its mainstream partners. Assange sent WikiLeaks spokesman Kristinn Hrafnsson and others to meet the newspapers to agree a deal. The newspapers – who were not told the full extent of WikiLeaks' self-publishing efforts – were reluctant to approve such a move but agreed to accept limited WikiLeaks self-publishing of material relating to Sweden and Iceland, plus any subject which had already been covered by the papers' publication schedule. Assange resolved after the meeting to stick to the agreement for the first few days of publication, and then publish wherever and whatever he wished. To an extent, this was the period in which WikiLeaks acted most like a traditional media organization. Its relationships with mainstream media partners, which it had come to view almost as rivals, were strained, and it intended to self-publish.

Unlike previous releases, the Embassy cables were hotly anticipated. In the weeks running up to the release, outlets across the world suggested potential content of the cables, publication dates and more. They were not alone. This time, the US State Department attempted to act first – apologizing to governments around the world, and warning them of material it believed would be contained in the cables, in addition to warning activists and others it believed might be at risk of being named in the documents.[11] The UK also acted ahead of publication of the cables, issuing a D-Notice – an advisory document for UK media organizations issued on rare occasions when stories might deal with sensitive material. Air Vice-Marshal Andrew Vallance cautioned editors:

> I understand that WikiLeaks will very shortly release a further mass of US official documents onto its Internet website. The full scope of the subject matter covered by these documents remains to be seen, but it is possible that some of them may contain information that falls within the UK's Defence Advisory Notice code. Given the large number of documents thought to be involved, it is unlikely

that sensitive UK national security information within
these documents would be recognized by a casual browser.
However, aspects of national security might be put at risk
if a major UK media news outlet brought such information
into obvious public prominence through its general publication or broadcast.

May I also ask you to bear in mind the potential conse-
quential effects of disclosing information which would put
at risk the safety and security of Britons working or living
in volatile regions where such publicity might trigger violent local reactions, for example Iran, Iraq, Pakistan and
Afghanistan?[12]

The government reaction prior to publication was greater
than that for any previous WikiLeaks release – but nothing
compared with what was to come.

On 28 November 2010, the first 220 of 251,857 Embassy
cables were published, alongside page after page of newspaper coverage, and led broadcasts across the world. Alongside
the first published cables, WikiLeaks wrote:

The embassy cables will be released in stages over the next
year. The subject matter of these cables is of such importance,
and the geographical spread so broad, that to do otherwise
would not do this material justice. The cables show the US
spying on its allies and the UN; turning a blind eye to corruption and human rights abuse in 'client states'; backroom deals
with supposedly neutral countries; lobbying for US corporations; and the measures US diplomats take to advance those
who have access to them. This document release reveals the
contradictions between the US's public persona and what
it says behind closed doors – and shows that if citizens in a
democracy want their governments to reflect their wishes,
they should ask to see what's going on behind the scenes.

The press impact was huge. According to Pew Research, one in four of all Twitter links were WikiLeaks-related, as were 16 per cent of all news links on blogs. For US consumers, the first week of WikiLeaks cables made up 16 per cent of all high-profile US news.[13]

The backlash was on a similar scale. WikiLeaks had expected – and received – condemnations from the White House, Department of Defense, and Department of State. The White House official statement said: 'Such disclosures put at risk our diplomats, intelligence professionals, and people around the world who come to the United States for assistance in promoting democracy and open government. President Obama supports responsible, accountable, and open government at home and around the world, but this reckless and dangerous action runs counter to that goal.'[14]

However, on this occasion, the backlash went still farther. WikiLeaks came under attack from pro-government hackers, one of whom – 'th3 j35t3r' – managed to briefly take the site offline ahead of the cables' publication. Such attacks led WikiLeaks to take extra webhosting from Amazon.com, who routinely offer such a service. When US Senator Joe Lieberman heard of this, he launched a furious condemnation of the move, leading Amazon to withdraw their servers, and then called on all other US businesses to do the same:

This morning Amazon informed my staff that it has ceased to host the WikiLeaks website. I wish that Amazon had taken this action earlier based on WikiLeaks' previous publication of classified material. The company's decision to cut off WikiLeaks now is the right decision and should set the standard for other companies WikiLeaks is using to distribute its illegally seized material. I call on any other company or organization that is hosting WikiLeaks to immediately terminate its relationship with them.

WikiLeaks' illegal, outrageous, and reckless acts have compromised our national security and put lives at risk around
the world. No responsible company – whether American or
foreign – should assist WikiLeaks in its efforts to disseminate these stolen materials.[15]

Lieberman's call was heeded: payment providers Visa,
Mastercard and PayPal all revoked WikiLeaks' account, leaving the organization, which had been raising over $100,000
a day in the immediate aftermath of the cables' publication, with virtually no means of raising funds. Other sites
which had hosted interactive graphics or other services for
WikiLeaks also cut them off. In retaliation, a hacker collective known as Anonymous vowed retaliation on WikiLeaks'
behalf.

The group – made up of hackers of varying ability, with
no formal structure, leadership or purpose – took retaliation through a series of 'denial of service' attacks against
the corporate websites of Mastercard and PayPal and even
of Senator Lieberman's and US government sites. Others
responded by voluntarily duplicating the WikiLeaks site on
their own webservers, in case the main site was taken down.
As a result, WikiLeaks is now duplicated live in more than
1,000 places across the Internet – though due to an apparent
coding error, WikiLeaks itself no longer lists the location of
these sites.

The scale of the online challenge between supporters of
WikiLeaks and supporters of the US government prompted
John Perry Barlow, founder of the Electronic Frontier
Foundation, to say: 'The first serious infowar is now engaged.
The field of battle is WikiLeaks. You are the troops.'[16]

Responding to such technical, public relations and legal
challenges alone was almost enough to push WikiLeaks to
the limit. On top of that they had to cope with the far more

complex daily publication schedule of cables for each of five newspapers – a daily schedule that proved far more complicated than the one-off method used for the Iraq and Afghan releases. However, it proved to be much more effective at increasing the quantity of coverage. Given this workload, WikiLeaks was managing to get only one or two stories a day published direct onto its own website.

Even this slowed after Julian Assange's Swedish sex case caught up with him as an international arrest warrant was issued. Police contacted Assange's lawyers to arrange for him to turn himself in for arrest. The date of 7 December was agreed. Assange arrived at the police station, was arrested and, to his own surprise – and that of his staff – was refused bail and remanded in custody.

WikiLeaks' challenges got still harder: the organization came under a yet more intense level of direct scrutiny, centred on whether it could even continue to function with Assange incarcerated. A WikiLeaks staffer made a furious phone call to a senior *Guardian* editor after the newspaper published a story questioning whether WikiLeaks would survive, only to be gently reminded that WikiLeaks was yet to put out a statement of its own in response to Assange's detention. The hastily drawn-up statement, put out in the name of spokesman Kristinn Hrafnsson, led several papers the next day, including (for one edition) the *Guardian*: 'This will not stifle WikiLeaks. The release of the US embassy cables – the biggest leak in history – will still continue. We will not be gagged, either by judicial action or corporate censorship.'

Assange was bailed to Vaughan Smith's manor just over a week later, though strict conditions including a curfew and requirement to sign in at the local police station, cut significantly into his working day. Preparations for his first extradition hearing took much of the remaining time.

Coupled with further internal tensions and the planned departure of many of the overseas journalists, WikiLeaks was left with more work to do and fewer people to do it. It continued to publish stories slowly in its own right, in addition to beginning work to broaden the number of international publishing partners with access to cables. It was this strand of work that proved most fruitful for WikiLeaks. Though work has been slower than Assange originally intended, more than eighty news organizations worldwide have now been given access to Embassy cables material by WikiLeaks.[17] While WikiLeaks has shown itself to be extraordinarily overstretched – and, to an extent, fragile – it has also to date endured more simultaneous sources of pressure than perhaps any other media organization worldwide has ever faced.

By this point WikiLeaks was routinely describing itself as a journalistic organization. It was gathering information and distributing it. It was editing that information and packaging its release. The significance lies in examining whether it offered new principles or practices for journalism and what it revealed about mainstream media. We will now look at some ethical and editorial issues as a way of understanding the challenges it posed.

## 2.5 RIGHTS, RISKS AND RESPONSIBILITIES

There is no such thing as perfect freedom of expression, and certainly media freedom has always been conditional. It is a trade-off between rights and responsibilities. Journalists have extra rights compared to ordinary citizens. In liberal democracies it varies from state to state, but there are usually special provisions in law to allow journalists additional access to information and the right to say things that other people want suppressed. In the UK, for example, the media have the right to report anything said by an MP in the Houses of

Parliament. Legal and constitutional guarantees of freedom of the press such as the American First Amendment are balanced with legal restrictions such as defamation or copyright legislation. There are also practical advantages granted to journalists, such as press facilities in courts or parliaments.

In return for these privileges, mainstream mass media journalism has, over time, offered various qualitative assurances, as well as accepting legal constraints. For example, the idea that journalism should attempt to report the truth objectively and fairly is a core rationale given for journalism's special status. In most liberal democracies this arrangement is overseen by relatively informal structures of self-regulation, usually mixed with legislative backing: editorial codes, professional standards, trades unions, industry councils, charters and ombudsmen.

WikiLeaks explicitly makes the claim to be a journalistic organization. Much of its self-description in this phase uses the mainstream ethical and editorial language of truth, rights and responsibility. Yet the debate around its collaboration with its mainstream media partners in this period showed how WikiLeaks remained at odds with aspects of the settlement between traditional journalism and society. WikiLeaks raises questions about the limits of disclosure and the right of authority to control information flows. It forces us to reconsider the responsibility of the journalist to avoid causing harm. It challenges us to think again about the degree to which mainstream news media have been willing and able to fulfil their responsibility for truth-telling. Perhaps most importantly, it questions whether mainstream media are culpable or commendable in their relationship with the state. Is traditional journalism able to carry out its responsibility to hold power to account in the Internet era? As we shall see in chapter 3, WikiLeaks is by no means alone in raising these issues. These are all questions that historically have been continually raised within mainstream media themselves. Other forms of alternative media have made this challenge throughout modern media history. But WikiLeaks poses those problems on a new scale and in fresh terms. By interacting with mainstream media it offers a new paradigmatic space for the interrogation of journalistic values. Let us now try to break down that general argument into specific areas of principles and practice.

## 2.6 THE RESPONSIBILITY OF JOURNALISM TO AVOID HARM

WikiLeaks and its mainstream media collaborators had different standards, attitudes and capacity for safeguarding people mentioned in the 2010 leaks. We have seen how at a practical level WikiLeaks relied on relatively instinctive personal judgements rather than research or expertise in making decisions about which names or facts were to be removed or redacted. According to his collaborators' account, Julian Assange was making a different ethical calculation about the risk posed by putting information into the public domain compared to his mainstream media partners. In the *Guardian*'s account of an early meeting with Assange, it quotes this response from Assange to their concern that informants in Afghanistan might be identified through the leaks and so face violent retribution from the Taliban: 'Well they're informants. So if they get killed, they've got it coming to them. They deserve it'[18] – although, as the *Guardian* account also acknowledges, Assange did review that position and by the end of the process was acting like a 'mainstream publisher'.[19]

As soon as WikiLeaks accepted a responsibility to avoid harm, it had to consider the complexity of the risk that the journalism posed. First, there was a direct risk to individuals

who had put themselves in danger – for example, as informants. To describe what they had done or other circumstantial
detail would help in their identification, even if names were
edited out. They would be at risk of direct reprisal against
them or their families or associates. Likewise, there was the
general threat posed to (mainly American) armed forces.
Publishing details of their operational tactics and procedures would help their enemies to plan their attacks better.
Any criticism of the military campaign could be seen as
unpatriotic and could undermine support for actions that
a democratically elected administration had deemed in the
national interest.

With the cables release, the risk was mainly the unknown
consequences of disrupting the normal assumptions of confidentiality in diplomatic activity. There was the risk to
individual diplomats' careers. By revealing what they had said
candidly in private, WikiLeaks ended the tenure of several
American ambassadors, some of whom may have been doing
work to make the world a better place. For example, did the
fact that Carlos Pascual had to resign his post as ambassador
to Mexico help or hinder efforts to combat drug trafficking?
It is arguable that only one illegal action on the part of the
American government was revealed by the cables: the policy
of spying on UN officials.

In respect of other peoples' abuses, the cables often made
manifest what was previously unconfirmed officially, rather
than revealing a new malfeasance. So, for example, it was
widely suspected by Tunisians that President Ben Ali was
corrupt, but the publication of a US cable saying so gave
the allegation much greater authority and suggested that the
State Department might even be sympathetic to attempts to
unseat him.[20] However, by exposing American diplomatic
thinking, it is also possible that WikiLeaks compromised
American efforts to provide covert support to reformists.

Nothing discredits a Middle East liberal movement quicker than association with the US State Department.

Finally, there was the much more general potential harm of undermining the work of diplomats as an international system. Diplomats would argue that it is vital that they can assume that their communications – which are in effect the substance of their work – are private. In general, if diplomats cannot be candid in private, their effectiveness is inhibited. More specifically, certain kinds of diplomacy would be made much harder. For example, Norway has a long and successful history acting as a neutral diplomatic go-between in seemingly intractable disputes. One senior Norwegian diplomat told us that the threat of disclosure would seriously compromise the kind of work that brought about the Oslo Accords. So, even though the diplomatic cables were relatively low-level communications with a quite low security clearance, their publication had impacts that carried real risks. We still do not know what further risks are implicit in the unreleased cables or the rationale for keeping them out of the public eye.

In reality there has been little, if any, evidence that the leaks did direct harm to individuals, though it is debatable how, or whether, we would ever know if someone had suffered. Likewise, the more general damage to diplomacy would be hard to show empirically. The alleged Bradley Manning leak was a consequence of the US State Department increasing its information-sharing in the wake of 9/11 but officials characterize it as an exceptional mistake, by one part of the military/intelligence structure, that is not likely to be repeated. US officials said that diplomatic communications may become more restricted and reduced in volume but that might be an efficiency gain rather than a handicap to effective diplomacy.[21] Perhaps more significantly, the authorities appreciate and must adjust to the fact that they now operate in a context of greater potential exposure. We will look at the wider implications of that in chapter 3. Will it lead to greater transparency and accountability, or a clampdown on information, or simply greater uncertainty? That in itself is another risk calculation that flows from these publications.

## 2.7 RESPONSIBILITY TO TELL THE TRUTH

The most basic responsibility of any journalist is to make sure that the material they publish is accurate. Where there are facts, they should be correct. Related to that are responsibilities to ensure that the presentation is impartial and objective. These 'truths' are inevitably relative to the perspective of the journalist, the audience and the context, but the assumption is that the journalist is striving towards that goal. If they are not, then they should make it clear that their report is partial, partisan or provisional. There is also the problem that there are specific and general truths. A fact out of context may be so misleading that the resultant report is in effect untrue. The act of journalism is a representation and therefore, in a sense, a distortion of reality. It always involves the selection of material and the presentation of it in a way that is framed by factors such as the journalist's ideology, commercial imperatives, resources of time and space, or cultural and political assumptions. Any journalistic narrative adopts a certain framing of an issue or event. This kind of relativism does not necessarily undermine the principle of truth-seeking. In fact it could be argued that relativism is at the heart of journalism itself. Journalism is an act of social communication, not science. All journalism is contestable and provisional but must still be principled. If it is to have an ethical claim, it cannot ignore the responsibility to an idea of the truth.

WikiLeaks did not ignore this responsibility. Julian

Assange is as likely to make truth claims as, say, Bill Keller of the *New York Times*. Interestingly, throughout its history, no one has ever questioned the authenticity of any document published by WikiLeaks. But in the larger sense, the manner in which WikiLeaks operated did challenge assumptions about exercising the responsibility of truth.

Originally WikiLeaks promised to publish everything sent to it that it could confirm as genuine. By 'genuine', it meant that the documents were authentic, and had been subject to some kind of verification process. This meant they sometimes even published material that was of little interest to the editorial managers of WikiLeaks. For example, Domscheit-Berg cites the series of American fraternity handbooks leaks which he and his colleagues considered were of little importance. They felt compelled to publish the secrets of these cultish American student societies, much to the chagrin of many college members, but it was hardly a fatal blow against global injustice or state violence.[22]

WikiLeaks validated documents in a very informal way. It seems that in the initial stages, few of the editorial checks and balances of mainstream media were observed. This kind of leaker-driven publication meant that the wider responsibility to objectivity and context was not observed by WikiLeaks regarding each specific leak. Clearly WikiLeaks was not acting as a mainstream media reporter. They were not present at the subject locations. The Collateral Murder investigation was an exception to this in that they did hire journalists to research background information. It is not clear what expertise they were able to draw upon in analysing the material they received either. Assange talked about a network of supporters who contributed, but there is little confirmation and even less evidence of any interpretive processing of the information involved. It raised the question – very much related to the question of responsibility:

did they know what they were doing? Had they any sense
of the specific consequences of what they were publishing,
based on a sophisticated understanding of the material itself?

Julian Assange has always been insistent on there being a
material truth. It is just that he thinks that it has been covered up. Like all their leaks, putting the Afghan logs / Iraq
war logs / Embassy cables into the public domain was an
attempt on WikiLeaks' part at 'pure' information disclosure.
The edited Collateral Murder video had been something
of a one-off experiment that was not followed up. Instead,
they went back to the extensive disclosure model. The aim
was that by providing such a volume of relatively unfil-
tered, unpackaged material, it would be possible to change
the accepted wisdom or received opinion on the nature of
America's wars. However, as we have seen, Assange's strategy now recognized that, with these leaks, there was too
much material, and that he needed a mainstream platform
to amplify its impact. In practice, that also meant adapting to
mainstream media procedures and values. Once WikiLeaks
accepted the need for redaction to avoid harm, for example,
they had compromised the purity of their mission. By collab-
orating with mainstream media they had gained a platform
but one that insisted on editing rights. To make the material meaningful and accessible, their professional partners
reworked it into colourful interactive graphs and selected
the juiciest quotes and prioritized the most dynamic stories.
The raw data were also made available, but even then, only a
small minority of the documents have been published so far.
At the same time, the documents that were used were put
online in their redacted versions so readers could search and
study the material for themselves.

Clearly WikiLeaks was now sharing a mainstream media
approach to the idea of truth by its association with its collaborators. The fact that it had an ideological motivation

does not distinguish it. It is very much a traditional aspect of campaigning journalism to pursue a higher moral or political 'truth'. In WikiLeaks' case, it was the belief that states like the USA were prone to a conspiracy to conceal injustice. However, in practice they now shared the relativism that comes with any act of editing and selection.

## 2.8 RESPONSIBILITY TO HOLD POWER TO ACCOUNT

A fundamental justification of journalism's privileges, and its value generally, is that it is an essential part of the democratic process. The so-called 'fourth estate' is there as an institutional power that can prevent the abuse of authority. WikiLeaks' partners on the Afghan/Iraq/Embassy stories all claim great traditions of fulfilling that role. Mainstream media hold power to account on a continual basis and in various ways at different levels. By giving the public information about the operations of government, business and other organizations, they help citizens to monitor those who have influence on their lives. By publishing analysis and comment, they provide a forum for power to enter into dialogue with the citizen. But they also have a responsibility to produce journalism that is critical and challenging, and to investigate the workings of power. They can work to destroy those who have power and change the way it operates, against the will of those in authority. Part of this aspect is to reveal information that power would prefer to keep secret. A liberal democratic journalism can strive to be impartial but it cannot simply replicate consensus. If journalism does not ask tough questions, offer alternatives and expose failings of power, then it cannot be said to be fulfilling its wider watchdog role. But this means that it must take risks, provoke censure and create disagreement. All mainstream media editors would agree, in that sense, with Julian Assange when he says that 'if journalism is good, it is controversial'.[23] Assange himself sees WikiLeaks in the journalism tradition as part of a fourth estate: 'WikiLeaks remains true to the ideals of the popular newspapers that flourished in the US at the beginning of the 20th century. . . . These newspapers not only reported the news but also offered . . . a venue where readers could debate political, economics and cultural issues.'[24]

The debate has always been about the degree of power that the fourth estate enjoys relative to those in authority when it fulfils this function, and how far it should go to be disruptive and destabilizing of authority. There is a long history of journalists and others who argue that the news media are severely restricted in their ability to hold power to account. For example, Philip Knightley has described how journalism is particularly subject to direct control and manipulation during times of conflict.[25] In a much more general sense, Noam Chomsky, along with his co-author Ed Herman, is one of many media analysts who have pointed out the degree to which mainstream media can be complicit in 'manufacturing consent'.[26] Chomsky does not assert a deliberate conspiracy as such, but Assange appears to be echoing the structural political analysis when he describes a 'conspiracy'.[27] Mainstream media and those in power know each other. They share schools and dining tables. To function, mass media must in practice rely on power for regular information. In many cases they rely directly or indirectly on power for revenue – from taxation or advertising, for example. In political journalism most scoops are the product of deliberate, selective leaking by those in power, rather than the disclosure of information through independent whistle-blowers. The UK MPs' expenses scandal was a rare example of a major case of the latter. However, it also begged the question of why the issue had never been raised before except by investigators outside of mainstream media like the freelance investigative journalist Heather Brooke and the political transparency website mySociety. MySociety director Tom Steinberg pointed out how the critical move to prevent the MPs concealing their expenses was secured by pressure from social not mainstream media:

> Over 7000 people joined a Facebook group, they sent thousands of emails to over 90 per cent of all MPs. Hundreds of thousands of people found out about the story by visiting TheyWorkForYou to find something they wanted to know, reading an email alert, or simply discovered what was going on whilst checking their Facebook or Twitter pages. Almost all of this happened, from nowhere, within 48 hours, putting enough pressure on Parliament to force change. Make no mistake. This is new, and it reflects the fact that the Internet generation expects information to be made available, and they expect to be able to make up their own minds, not be spoon-fed the views of others. This campaign was always about more than receipts, it was about changing the direction of travel, away from secrecy and towards openness.[28]

This is not to say that mainstream media are entirely compliant, but simply to point out that in any mutual systematic relationship there is bound to be a danger of what has been called Group Think, and that alternative forms of political communication can offer more challenging ways to hold power to account.

One of the factors that condition mainstream media behaviour is the knowledge that they are part of the wider societies they report on. Journalists are notorious for short-termism, but there is an institutional memory, a historical awareness of the consequences of their actions. This can promote as well as inhibit the quest for truth or the critique of authority.

The mainstream media institution can provide legal and economic protection for the risk-taking, truth-seeking journalist. The journalistic institution also offers cultural support in the sense of an institutional editorial policy. It may have a declared set of guidelines, a code, or a political stance and a brand that help the audience to recognize and trust that particular publication source. So, as an institution, it is aware of its public role. In other words, it is aware that it has power:

> To have that power news organizations need to be organizations – which have a collective memory, a clear goal, ideals, a commercial department which preserves or enhances their power by increasing their reach and influence, a legal department which will protect them from legal challenge, a training and mentoring facility which brings their staff up to the required levels of competence and increasingly retrains them in the use of changing technology, a reputation in the world which will assist reporters to gain entrance and have calls taken, a career structure and a pension plan . . . That is, such organizations professionalise the collection of news, and thus give it a structure.[29]

However, it is that organizational relationship to power for the mainstream media institution that can mean that the institutional pressures work against certain kinds of journalism. They can also inhibit independence and a risk-taking, critical approach. The fourth estate is by definition in a relationship with the other estates that is not always critical and distanced. That is how you get individuals like Judith Miller of the *New York Times* helping to fuel the WMD scare that led to the Iraq War. As the *Times'* editor Bill Keller recognized in a note that reviewed its coverage, her misreporting was part of a collective, institutional error:

> Some critics of our coverage during that time have focused blame on individual reporters. Our examination, however, indicates that the problem was more complicated. Editors at several levels who should have been challenging reporters and pressing for more skepticism were perhaps too intent on rushing scoops into the paper. Accounts of Iraqi defectors were not always weighed against their strong desire to have Saddam Hussein ousted. Articles based on dire claims about Iraq tended to get prominent display, while follow-up articles that called the original ones into question were sometimes buried. In some cases, there was no follow-up at all.[30]

In this admirable act of self-criticism, Keller went some way to showing the value of a news institution in correcting its own institutional flaws, however unusual that might be.

Despite its increasing collaboration with mainstream media institutions like the *New York Times*, WikiLeaks remained a stateless organization with its own internal logic. It has a declared responsibility to truth, but without the conditionality of mainstream media's similar claim. WikiLeaks remained without the commercial or constitutional context of its partners. If it had an institutional culture or ethos, it remained largely internalized and mainly embodied in Assange himself. That fundamental difference allows it to live with – if not reconcile – the contradiction between its avowed alternative ideology outside of the 'conspiracy' of the state and its collaboration and compromises with mainstream media.

Particularly in this phase of the Afghan/Iraq/Embassy leaks, WikiLeaks exposed the limits of some conventional media in holding power to account. WikiLeaks showed that investigative journalism could go much further using the new technologies, in both gathering information and its dissemination. It showed how little we are told about the inner workings of the military and diplomatic systems. It demonstrated the degree to which authority patronizes the public and seeks to control public discourse. If so much of the information in the cables was harmless, then why conceal it?

In the last decades in the West there have been rising levels of public scepticism about the operation of power and the integrity of those who have it. This has been fuelled by many factors, such as improved education and increased individualism combined with a loss of the deference previously fostered, for example, by organized religion. But this has not necessarily been matched by an increased critical ability within mainstream media. Some commentators argue that mainstream media have become too cynical. They argue that the automatic assumption of mendacity in politicians, for example, is poisoning public discourse. There may be some truth in this. Certainly, in some mainstream media there is a default assumption of base motives on the part of those in power. However, the evidence of WikiLeaks suggests that the problem may be that mainstream media are not sceptical enough – or at least not intelligent and persistent in their inquiries. There appear to be whole areas of foreign and military policy especially where the mainstream media have not been effective in producing the evidence to hold power to account. The Afghan and Iraq leaks showed that America had not been honest about the conduct of the war and its failures. It lied about the use of torture, the civilian deaths and the lack of success. Other mainstream journalists have told parts of that story but only WikiLeaks was able to tell it so comprehensively and irrefutably. The fact that mainstream media did provide a platform for these leaks showed that they are prepared to tell those stories, albeit on their own terms. But it raises the question of whether WikiLeaks opens up new possibilities for accountability journalism or simply constitutes an exceptional episode. We'll look at that in chapter 3.

In the debate about holding power to account and the role of the media in the public sphere, it may be that Julian Assange is quite a conventional media idealist.[31] He does believe that journalism can create an informed society that can facilitate progressive political change. But if journalism is to be part of a political process, then does it also have a responsibility to be held to account itself? As we have seen, there are mechanisms and conventions in most liberal democracies to oversee mainstream media, as well as general and specific legislation. WikiLeaks is institutionally outside of that framework despite its dealings with mainstream media. However, there are reasons why it should be accountable and they are all to do with trust. There is a great amount of cant spoken and written about trust in journalism,[32] but, as we shall discuss in more detail in chapter 4, it is increasingly the basic currency of communications online. The Internet offers the potential for transparency as the default. If all journalism is open to comment and reaction online, then it becomes increasingly accountable to a de facto right of reply and a boundless sphere of criticism. The degree to which that happens effectively depends on having open journalism and an open Internet, but the infrastructure is there. Increasingly, the public assume a degree of interactivity that allows this to happen. They might not always avail themselves of it, but having the option is essential to assuring a degree of trust. So it is a paradox that WikiLeaks, which takes advantage of the Internet's ability to hold power to account in a radically open way, is itself not open. By the standards of the Internet as well as conventional journalism, WikiLeaks is not accountable.

WikiLeaks publishes no financial accounts or annual reports. It does not answer questions about income, employees or structure. It does not have any accountability mechanism or governance structure. It does not show its internal workings or give a right of reply. It does not engage in a debate about its strategy either. In its early history, WikiLeaks suggested it would seek to expose authoritarian states, yet more recently the target of the leaking, if not its content, has been America. Specific queries are not dealt with openly, such as its relationship to 'Israel Shamir', an anti-Semitic Holocaust denier and someone who allegedly handed over WikiLeaks documents to the authoritarian rulers of Belorussia. The UK freedom-of-expression NGO Index on Censorship was concerned that 'Shamir has used his access to the WikiLeaks' US diplomatic cables to aid the prosecution of civil society activists within Belarus.'[33]

When a whole series of questions were put to WikiLeaks, the reply was simply: 'We have no further reports on this "rumour/issue".'

WikiLeaks might argue that it is necessarily secretive. Most obviously, it must protect its sources. Its infrastructure has come under technical attack and economic pressure. But the culture of non-accountability lays it open to the charge of hypocrisy. It criticizes governments and mainstream media for their lack of openness. It claims to be a transparency organization but it is not fully transparent itself. It is arguable that WikiLeaks should be more, not less, accountable than those it critiques. This reduces WikiLeaks' political impact. Those it accuses can accuse WikiLeaks of being secretive and conspiratorial. This in turn will damage its credibility with the public who both support its work and have the power to use the information to effect change. A lack of accountability can also reduce long-term editorial sustainability. In the networked communications environment, if you are not open then other people will hold you to account. If are not openly credible or trusted, then other organizations will not connect to you. This is critical for WikiLeaks, which relies on widespread public support for financing but also for amplifying its message and protecting it from extreme action by hostile governments. Instead of accepting responsibility for accountability, WikiLeaks has adopted the posture of the victim. It appears to plead that it is a vulnerable alternative political group rather than the powerful media organization it has become.

## 2.9 CONCLUSION

So we can see that this latest phase of WikiLeaks activities has taken it to an inherently contradictory position where it may have to make significant choices. By the middle of 2011 WikiLeaks was still not accepting fresh leaks as it was working at capacity to process the diplomatic cables. But barring a catastrophic event, it will continue. However, by the end of 2010 it had shifted its model from an alternative to a networked media organization. Its ethical basis and practice had itself been challenged. The outsider journalist had to an extent been brought into the mainstream. WikiLeaks hoped to profit from the disintermediation of news by connecting directly with the public. In the end it connected most successfully to a mass audience when it worked with mainstream media that already had access to a large-scale consumer base. By doing so it also changed its publication style to one that incorporated information with context and explanation. That shift seemed to suggest that the global audience still enjoys the efficiencies of more traditional editorial production alongside the potential for new forms of political communication through social media and the Internet.

The threat to authority had been accommodated. The

potential for disruption had been partially realized but, to have any significant impact on the nature of power, it has to be sustainable over time. To achieve that requires more than protection and revenue. As this phase showed, it also needs credibility and a much more sustainable editorial and organizational practice. What this phase of WikiLeaks also shows us is that journalism itself is now changing. As we shall examine in chapters 3 and 4, there is a further responsibility for journalism – and that is to adapt to the new networked age with an ethical framework.

# 3

# WIKILEAKS AND THE FUTURE OF JOURNALISM

## 3.1 INTRODUCTION

The arrest of Julian Assange by the British police on 7 December 2010 was the moment when the news narrative around WikiLeaks shifted directly to the personal. His fight to avoid extradition and the show of solidarity by his supporters meant that the ensuing legal struggle was centre-stage in the drama of WikiLeaks' future. This coincided with the period from autumn 2010 when divisions within WikiLeaks were made explicit through the departure of key figures like Daniel Domscheit-Berg, who also published a critical memoir.[1] The *Guardian*, which had been WikiLeaks' partner, also rushed to bring out a book on WikiLeaks which contained significant allegations of unethical and eccentric behaviour on the part of Julian Assange personally, as well as implicit criticisms of WikiLeaks as an organization.[2] This book sealed the rift between the two organizations, which were probably as close ideologically as any mainstream and alternative media entities could be. As we saw in chapter 2, the relationship between WikiLeaks' collaborators was strained and this came to the fore during a difficult phase for Assange personally. He challenged many of the criticisms and even threatened legal action against the *Guardian*, several of its staff, and Daniel Domscheit-Berg. The man whose own organization had sidestepped so many legal sanctions was now apparently prepared to use the courts against former partners.

Unlike many of his critics, Julian Assange saw no disconnect or irony in these actions. In his view, actions against WikiLeaks were an assault on the right to freedom of speech against governments who want to squash dissent. Whereas his own threatened legal actions – none of which had materialized at the time of writing – related to personal smears against his reputation.

The allegations within the *Guardian* material that drew his particular ire centred on his attitude towards those named in the reporting of the cables. The *Guardian* book[3] contended that at a meeting with reporters from that paper and *Der Spiegel*, Assange had said those named in the documents were 'collaborators' who deserved any consequences they would face if their information was made public. He has publicly denied these claims, but has also said in front of staff from the UK's Bureau of Investigative Journalism and Sweden's SVT channel that any deaths resulting from the publication of documents would be justified in the pursuit of 'greater good'. As we have seen, Assange also complained about the use of leaked documents from WikiLeaks relating to Israel Shamir, a known anti-Semite and defender of dictators including Belarus' Lukashenko, who was deeply involved in the distribution of Eastern European and Russian diplomatic cables for WikiLeaks. WikiLeaks persistently downplayed Shamir's involvement, but the *Guardian* published documents showing Shamir had invoiced the organization for payment, and had been entrusted with distributing WikiLeaks material. Shamir, the book revealed, had even stayed with Assange in the run-up to the cables' publication.[4]

This was a period of high drama, but what does it tell us about the significance of WikiLeaks? The (almost) unravelling of WikiLeaks from the autumn of 2010 showed that the organization was inherently unstable but also remarkably resilient. Despite the personal difficulties of its 'chief excecutive', it continued to publish material, although at mid-2011 it was still not accepting new leaks. In that sense, it was living off its archive: almost entirely the material believed to have originated from Bradley Manning.

Control and distribution of the Manning material was becoming a growing problem for WikiLeaks. With submissions closed, the organization's reliance on this was growing, but WikiLeaks' control over it was slipping. As early as October 2010, UK freedom-of-information campaigner Heather Brooke had obtained a full copy of the Embassy cables from an ex-WikiLeaks source, but chose not to distribute these independently, instead working with the *Guardian*. In the following months, Norwegian newspaper *Aftenpost* also obtained a full copy of the cables without Assange's consent. Tranches of cables turned up as far afield as Lebanon, where *Al Akhbar* obtained several hundred cables without WikiLeaks' knowledge, though Assange later claimed credit for it.

By the release of the last set of documents obtained from Manning – the prisoner records of the 779 individuals detained at Guantánamo Bay – WikiLeaks' loss of control of its documents for the first time nearly jeopardized the organization's ability to scoop the mainstream media. WikiLeaks had once again built a global coalition of media partners. The *Guardian* and *New York Times*, as a result of their soured relationship, were excluded, replaced in their respective countries by the *Daily Telegraph* and the *Washington Post*. However, without WikiLeaks' knowledge, the *Guardian* and *New York Times* had obtained the Guantánamo papers and prepared them for release in April 2011, weeks ahead of the proposed publication date of WikiLeaks' new partners. Assange learned of the move just hours ahead of publication, leading to a scramble of his new coalition to get the material out. WikiLeaks managed to publish the files in part on the same day, and in full two days after the *Guardian* and *New York Times* went live, somewhat recovering its position.

By managing, even if just barely, to see through the release of the Guantánamo papers successfully, coupled with a carefully rationed distribution of Embassy cables to outlets across the world, WikiLeaks managed to continue its publication run in the first half of 2011 despite a lack of new material and funds, and mounting political pressure.

At the same time, WikiLeaks had become a rallying point for a range of political groups and individuals. During a panel debate in London[5] Julian Assange was being criticized by conservative commentator Douglas Murray for undermining trust in mainstream democratic institutions. A heckler in the 800-strong and fervently pro-WikiLeaks crowd shouted out, 'that's WHY we like him, it's because we DON'T trust you lot!' In this sceptical age, WikiLeaks taps into a general distrust of authority and a decline in deference. It also draws strong support from more overtly anti-establishment, anti-corporate, anti-American groups, often but not exclusively of the Left. Libertarians and even Fox News have been enthusiastic at times. The group of supporters in London directly supporting Assange personally at this time were mixed. They included former soldier and TV news cameraman turned journalism club proprietor Vaughan Smith, left-wing investigative journalist John Pilger, and heiress Jemima Khan. WikiLeaks was now a cause as well as a media organization.

The public debate around the allegations of sexual misconduct by Julian Assange were one example of this process at work. In this book we have not dealt with them in detail because they are part of a continuing legal process but also because, in themselves, they are not relevant to an analysis of the significance of WikiLeaks. However, the allegations and the legal proceedings were an opportunity for people with differing views on WikiLeaks to take sides. In supporting Assange's legal efforts or in criticizing those who brought the charges, people demonstrated how partisan feelings had become about Assange and WikiLeaks. Some Assange supporters claimed that the criminal process had been instigated and prolonged by individuals and authorities keen to damage WikiLeaks. These supporters made a range of accusations including over-zealous 'media feminism',[6] intelligence agency conspiracies and judicial arbitrariness. The critics attacked Assange, according to John Pilger, because WikiLeaks is dangerous: 'The attacks on WikiLeaks and its founder, Julian Assange, are a response to an information revolution that threatens old power orders, in politics and journalism.'[7] However, critics such as feminist journalist Libby Brooks said that claim was being used as an excuse to avoid taking the charges seriously:

Assange's status as embattled warrior for free speech is taken as giving permission – by those on the left as well as right – to indulge in the basest slut-shaming and misogyny. It's terrifying to witness how swiftly rape orthodoxies reassert themselves: that impugning a man's sexual propriety is a political act, that sexual assault complainants are prone to a level of mendacity others are not (and, in this case, deserving of the same crowd-sourced scrutiny afforded leaked diplomatic cables.)[8]

This all personalized the debate around WikiLeaks in the figure of Assange. This personalization does not seem, in general, to be something that he sought to avoid: 'I am the heart and soul of this organization, its founder, philosopher, spokesperson, original coder, organizer, financier, and all the rest.'[9]

WikiLeaks was originally highly identified with Assange and this drama did little to dispel the idea that it was still a Single Person Organization, a relatively common phenomenon in alternative media according to media theorists:

> Like small and medium-sized businesses, the founder cannot be voted out, and, unlike many collectives, leadership does not rotate. This is not an uncommon feature within organizations, irrespective of whether they operate in the realm of politics, culture or the 'civil society' sector. SPOs are recognizable, exciting, inspiring, and easy to feature in the media. Their sustainability, however, is largely dependent on the actions of their charismatic leader, and their functioning is difficult to reconcile with democratic values. This is also why they are difficult to replicate and do not scale up easily.[10]

So we can see how any discussion of WikiLeaks' future is bound up with 'what Julian wants'. It underlines how an organization without a governance structure, code, mission statement or accountability mechanism will inevitably be considered in relation to the declared ethics and ideas of its most prominent individual member. In that sense, Assange is WikiLeaks and so his personality does condition the wider analysis. Some opinions of Assange's character managed to combine admiration and disdain: 'I have never known such an extreme person as Julian Assange. So imaginative. So energetic. So brilliant. So paranoid, so power-hungry, so megalomanic.'[11]

Innovators and renegades in the media are rarely personalities who conform to conventional social norms. Even traditional investigative journalists are exceptionally motivated to practise their trade in its most arduous and often least popular form. This often means they are odd characters, especially when politically driven: 'I don't like Julian Assange's goals and methods, but corrective reformers are mostly unlikable weirdos.'[12]

This confluence of the personal and the public perhaps reached its most intense moment when the leaker was leaked. The *Guardian* published confidential court documents that detailed the accusations against Assange.[13] When, in a series of interviews,[14] Assange complained about this, it was perhaps not surprising that he was accused of hypocrisy by the mainstream media.[15]

That individual psychology has to be taken into account as, in this chapter, we will seek to place WikiLeaks' significance in the wider context of the future for new forms of investigative, disruptive and political journalism. This will be a more theoretical consideration of WikiLeaks as an organization and its significance, but lurking behind it remains the unusual personality of Assange himself. One of WikiLeaks' disruptive strengths is its unpredictability. Assange in some ways embodies that uncertainty principle.

In this chapter, Assange will remain at the centre of the analysis, but we will now try to put WikiLeaks and its future into a wider context. We will first look at WikiLeaks as part of the struggle to define the way that the Internet allows for the open distribution of information. In a sense this is about the eternal battle between those in power, with an interest in controlling information, and the journalist and citizen who wants it to be free. WikiLeaks is the subject of this argument about the open Internet, but also a significant actor in determining what happens. Then we will look at WikiLeaks as a model for imitators and adaptors of some of its principles and practices. What forms of journalism is WikiLeaks inspiring? What impact is it having on other kinds of journalism?

## 3.2 WIKILEAKS AS PART OF THE BATTLE FOR THE OPEN NET

Part of the significance of WikiLeaks in the future will be what it represents in terms of the struggle to maintain an open Internet. It is a case study of what is happening and so a good subject for the debate about the principles and policies that will govern cyberspace. It is one location for the power struggle that is emerging over the nature of the global digital public sphere.

We saw in chapter 2 how there was a concerted attack upon WikiLeaks following the major leaks of 2010. It was described as a 'terrorist' organization, and calls were even made for the assassination of Assange. US Vice President Joe Biden was the most senior of politicians to describe WikiLeaks as a threat: 'I would argue that it's closer to being a hi-tech terrorist. This guy has done things and put in jeopardy the lives and occupations of people in other parts of the world. He's made it difficult to conduct our business with our allies and our friends . . . It has done damage.'[16]

The US Justice Department has begun an active criminal investigation and has considered charges under the Espionage Act. A federal Grand Jury has begun investigating the possibility of prosecution, but, as it meets in secret, it is difficult to tell what the line of inquiry and the terms of the case might be.[17] Prosecution would be difficult because of the First Amendment protections for journalists, even when they re-publish illegally released material. Nor is it clear how the US Espionage Act might apply to an Australian. Some commentators have described the actions taken by the US Federal Government as a 'fishing expedition' designed to flush out activists and to intimidate supporters of groups like WikiLeaks.[18] However, considering the scale of the security breach, the current inquiries may be exceptional, but they are not necessarily disproportionate in the context of mainstream Washington politics. It is difficult to imagine how the American authorities could not have instituted some kind of legal process after such a significant illicit action. How hard they can or will pursue this in practice is another matter.

What was more unusual than the American government response was the reaction by private companies who provided services for WikiLeaks. Amazon ended its agreement to provide server space, although WikiLeaks was able to find alternative facilities. Visa, PayPal and other banks no longer provided payments services, so making fund-raising harder, though not impossible, for WikiLeaks. In June 2011 WikiLeaks claimed these actions had cost it $15m in donations. The number, based on an assumption that WikiLeaks would receive its highest one-day donation total every day that its payment providers had been unavailable, might be implausible, but it shows the importance the organization placed on the private blockade.

There is no evidence that the American government directly instigated the actions of these companies against WikiLeaks. The office of Senator Joe Lieberman admitted that publicity following his remarks may have played a part in the corporate decisions to stop hosting WikiLeaks servers and fund-raising systems. Certainly one of his aides had contact with Amazon.[19] However, it is claimed that there was no direct communication between government and the companies. The companies argued that WikiLeaks was in breach of their User Service Agreements. While their actions may have been justified under the letter of those agreements, it seems odd that WikiLeaks, rather than other criminally suspect organizations, has had its facilities terminated. WikiLeaks' supporters highlighted organizations including the Ku Klux Klan as those Visa and Mastercard were willing to supply. News organizations that had worked with WikiLeaks were also unaffected. The episode seemed to confirm fears that the curtailment of unrestricted communications on the Internet will occur indirectly through corporate as much as government actions.

Despite setting out a wider global agenda for an open Internet, the Obama administration did nothing to discourage those corporations who control the Internet's infrastructure from acting in a way that made WikiLeaks' journalism harder to publish. As we have pointed out, the whole point about WikiLeaks' fundamental exceptionalism is that it is outside of a specific geographical legal framework. This gives it a large degree of immunity from normal legal sanctions on the media. However, it could be argued that it also makes it ethically and practically harder for WikiLeaks to claim the protective rights enjoyed by mainstream media. In addition, some make the case that the WikiLeaks approach of having its freedom of expression cake and eating it could backfire for those organizations that remain within the traditional state/journalism compact. American First Amendment specialist lawyer Floyd Abrams acted for the *New York Times* in the Pentagon Papers case in the 1970s but he said that WikiLeaks may have, at best, killed off chances of a new law to extend protection for journalists and, at worst, precipitated a more censorious backlash:

> Mr Assange is no boon to American journalists. His activities have already doomed proposed federal shield-law legislation protecting journalists' use of confidential sources in the just-adjourned Congress. An indictment of him could be followed by the judicial articulation of far more speech-limiting legal principles than currently exist with respect to

even the most responsible reporting about both diplomacy and defense. If he is not charged or is acquitted of whatever charges may be made, that may well lead to the adoption of new and dangerously restrictive legislation. In more than one way, Mr. Assange may yet have much to answer for.[20]

This view has validity in the American political context. It may well be that in the short-term it will be harder to press for greater protection for journalists who obtain classified information through illicit channels. It would be easy to dismiss this as the inevitable reactionary backlash by a patriotic legislature that resents the assault on its national security. However, there is a deeper problem going forward for WikiLeaks, and disruptive journalism in general, in their relationship with the state in the Internet era. Abrams contrasts the selective leaking by Daniel Ellsberg, who withheld sensitive diplomatic documents, with what he sees as the wholesale alleged handover of information by Bradley Manning to WikiLeaks. The implication is that WikiLeaks has not been discriminating in its disclosures. And yet, WikiLeaks has also been selective in its release of the diplomatic cables. However, the rationale for selection was not to avoid harm to American foreign policy. WikiLeaks' principles were not aligned with national interest in the way that, say, the *New York Times* felt obliged to consult with the US government. WikiLeaks' eventual acceptance of thorough-going redaction was not entirely voluntary. Instead, as we saw in chapter 2, it was part of the process of accommodation to the editorial principles of its mainstream media partners. Yet even the *New York Times* editor Bill Keller, who felt real disquiet at Assange's ethics, still felt that WikiLeaks' actions merited protection:

> while I do not regard Assange as a partner, and I would hesitate to describe what WikiLeaks does as journalism, it

is chilling to contemplate the possible government prosecution of WikiLeaks for making secrets public, let alone the passage of new laws to punish the dissemination of classified information.[21]

Keller may hesitate to describe what WikiLeaks does as journalism, with all the cultural and political assumptions that the editor of a great mainstream newspaper would associate with that term. Few news organizations match the *New York Times* as an embodiment of mainstream, commercial journalism as an institution, constantly in tension between the dynamic of its reflective, critical faculties and the inertia of its historic capital and established social and political roles. However, WikiLeaks is not the *New York Times*, but it is an example of a new kind of journalistic act made possible by the Internet.

In the wider context, the problem for American and other legislators in the liberal democracies now goes beyond the traditional balancing of powers between the fourth estate and government. In political terms, WikiLeaks is a typical Internet phenomenon in the way that it disintermediates the relationship between government and the public. It enables the citizen to access government data without the mediating influence of mainstream journalism. So the news business faces the danger of losing its classic role as the conduit for information and the arbiter of critical processes that hold power to account. This makes it harder for the nation state to establish the rules of engagement. The wider question in the digital age then becomes how to reconcile support for this liberating potential of the Internet with the threat to the security of government information systems. So is WikiLeaks 'another example of the Internet overthrowing our settled habits? ... By this formulation, WikiLeaks is to the state and corporations what Napster was to music or Google to media-as-a-business.'[22]

The challenge for government and the news media is how to cope with the variable geometry of journalism and regulation on the Internet. Before WikiLeaks, there was a relatively level playing field for different media organizations across different platforms or genres. Now there are different laws or rules for the various organizations that operate in the same space. Apart from national differences, there are those that are willingly subject to state regulation and those, like WikiLeaks, that operate beyond national boundaries. Another example was the role in spring 2011 in the United Kingdom of the micro-blogging site Twitter in undermining the use of injunctions by celebrities.[23] So-called 'superinjunctions' were being used to create a blanket ban on any media reference to stories that were deemed by a judge to be private and beyond public interest. The media were not even allowed to report the existence of these superinjunctions. However, details did emerge through the Internet and especially on Twitter, allowing the British tabloid newspapers to argue that the facts were now in the public domain and so reportable. The British government is now reviewing the whole basis of privacy legislation and the role of the courts in setting the terms of media freedoms. It is another example of how an open Internet is a challenge, if not a contradiction, to the idea of national limits on freedom of expression.

There are broadly two sources of the threats to the open Internet for journalism. First, there is the threat of state regulation: censorship and control mainly motivated by a desire to suppress dissent and to protect privacy. There is also state censorship related to national security, especially at times of war. Second, there is the possibility that corporate interests – especially those that help to provide the infrastructure for the Internet – could adopt policies and support government actions that allow for a more restricted Internet. They might do this to gain the benefits of collaboration with government or for commercial advantage. Either trend would potentially compromise the communicative power of the Internet in general, and WikiLeaks-type disruptive journalism in particular.

What WikiLeaks does is journalism and, therefore, is part of any liberal democratic settlement for the Internet Age. This is the legal judgement that WikiLeaks supporter and media law professor Yochai Benkler has shown is the base of its defence as journalism in American law: 'We hold that individuals are journalists when engaged in investigative reporting, gathering news, and have the intent at the beginning of the news-gathering process to disseminate this information to the public.'[24]

As Benkler goes on to point out:

> The critical definitional element here is intent at the time of gathering and function, not mode of dissemination: intent to gather for public dissemination. There simply cannot be the remotest doubt that the entire purpose of WikiLeaks is the gathering of information for public dissemination; and the use of traditional media outlets as the primary pathway emphasizes this fact, although it is not constitutive or a necessary element of the defense. The professionalism, niceness, or personal hygiene of the reporter are not germane to the inquiry.[25]

This very American defence of free speech was given global expression by US Secretary of State Hillary Clinton in her seminal speech that established this principle as a vital part of the new digital world order and something that should be looked on as a human right:

> We stand for a single Internet where all of humanity has equal access to knowledge and ideas. And we recognize that

the world's information infrastructure will become what we and others make of it. Now, this challenge may be new, but our responsibility to help ensure the free exchange of ideas goes back to the birth of our republic. The words of the First Amendment to our Constitution are carved in 50 tons of Tennessee marble on the front of this building.[26]

At the same time she outlined how Internet freedom, like any other, is conditional: 'Those who use the Internet to recruit terrorists or distribute stolen intellectual property cannot divorce their online actions from their real world identities. But these challenges must not become an excuse for governments to systematically violate the rights and privacy of those who use the Internet for peaceful political purposes.'[27]

A year on, Hillary Clinton updated that statement in the wake of both the WikiLeaks controversy and the uprisings across the Arab world. She spoke of how the Internet was an agent for freedom but also recognized the relatively neutral nature of the technology itself:

There is a debate currently underway in some circles about whether the Internet is a force for liberation or repression. But I think that debate is largely beside the point. Egypt isn't inspiring people because they communicated using Twitter. It is inspiring because people came together and persisted in demanding a better future. Iran isn't awful because the authorities used Facebook to shadow and capture members of the opposition. Iran is awful because it is a government that routinely violates the rights of its people.[28]

So for Clinton the Internet is a remarkable new technology, but still subject to conventional power politics. When considered in policy terms it requires an agreed international framework to sustain the open Internet. At the same time her department was also interventionist in promoting the freedom of expression through direct investment in initiatives that would help in circumventing Internet censorship by other states:

> We are taking a venture capital-style approach, supporting a portfolio of technologies, tools, and training, and adapting as more users shift to mobile devices. We have our ear to the ground, talking to digital activists about where they need help, and our diversified approach means we're able to adapt the range of threats that they face. We support multiple tools, so if repressive governments figure out how to target one, others are available.[29]

So how is this reconciled with the hostility to WikiLeaks? At the same time, she made it clear that her criticism of WikiLeaks was based not on its use of the Internet for disclosure, but on the fact that it had handled stolen government property:

> I know that government confidentiality has been a topic of debate during the past few months because of WikiLeaks, but it's been a false debate in many ways. Fundamentally, the WikiLeaks incident began with an act of theft. Government documents were stolen, just the same as if they had been smuggled out in a briefcase. Some have suggested that this theft was justified because governments have a responsibility to conduct all of our work out in the open in the full view of our citizens. I respectfully disagree. The United States could neither provide for our citizens' security nor promote the cause of human rights and democracy around the world if we had to make public every step of our efforts. Confidential communication gives our

government the opportunity to do work that could not be done otherwise.[30]

It is fairly easy to find relatively minor contradictions within this policy that critics would suggest show that the American approach to an open Internet has been compromised, even apart from the legal pursuit of WikiLeaks.[31] It has been suggested that the US was involved, for example, in cyber attacks on other states. The *New York Times* reported that America had been working with Israel on a computer virus, Stuxnet, that was used to disable computers running Iran's nuclear programme.[32] The Homeland Security Service is allowed to search electronic devices that allow access to the Internet, such as laptops, at US Customs – even where there are no suspicious circumstances.[33] Famously, the Federal government also told its employees not to access the diplomatic cables on WikiLeaks, thus denying its own staff further knowledge of a story that everyone else was able to access.[34] These are semi-anecdotal, separate incidents or policies in applied circumstances. However, Benkler alleges a further more general contradiction, in the American government's response to WikiLeaks in particular, between Hillary Clinton's asserted principles and actual practice – in what the administration did not do, rather than what it has done. A sin of omission as much as commission. It brings together the corporate as well as governmental threat to Internet openness. If the American government believes in the open Internet and thinks it should foster critical oversight of other states, why was it not more magnanimous about WikiLeaks' assault upon its own practices?:

At a minimum, on the background of these actions and the presence of public appeals from Lieberman, the continued refusal of the U.S. government to distance itself from these actions suggest that these acts of corporate vigilantism were undertaken with a wink and a nod from the federal government. Together, they present an image of a government able to circumvent normal constitutional protections to crack down on critics who use the networked public sphere. This occurs through informal systems of pressure and approval on market actors who are not themselves subject to the constitutional constraints. This extralegal public–private partnership allows an administration to achieve through a multi-system attack on critics results that would have been practically impossible to achieve within the bounds of the constitution and the requirements of legality.[35]

The reality may be less deliberately conspiratorial than Benkler suggests. It is possible that both corporations and the US government are internally conflicted over the open Internet. There is an ideological and pragmatic argument going on in places like the State Department, just as there is within the corporate affairs departments of companies such as Google or Facebook. Institutionally, their over-riding motives must be Realpolitik or profit, but strategy may conflict with tactics. The open Internet has advantages in terms both of business for corporations and of soft power for American foreign policy. However, as WikiLeaks shows, it also presents threats in the short term. The cyber-optimists working in the State Department '21st Century Statecraft' initiative[36] were undermined in their efforts to convince their diplomatic colleagues of the power of the Internet to deliver positive political outcomes by the WikiLeaks revelations. Internet sceptics within the foreign policy machine in Washington were emboldened by the Embassy cables release to question the wider wisdom of promoting an open Internet. They understood that it was a challenge to their institutional control of flows of information. Just two weeks before the WikiLeaks publications, Alec J. Ross, the State Department's digital guru, had spoken about the Internet, as 'the Che Guevara of the 21st Century'.[37] Not surprisingly, his more hard-nosed colleagues did not share his enthusiasm for this kind of revolution when it turned their own world upside-down.

The Arab uprisings in early 2011, partially facilitated by new communications technologies, helped to restore political credibility to the open Internet approach. Indeed, so much so that Ross was able to restate his association between political revolution and digital technologies: 'If hierarchies are being levelled then people at the top of those hierarchies are finding themselves on much shakier ground. What's remarkable is the speed, this is lightning fast change taking place and I've got to be honest, I think this is fun. It's going to be wildly disruptive in the next few years and I think this is a good thing.'[38] Within this wider enthusiasm for Internet-inspired change, the State Department has settled on an instrumentalist approach to digital communications. It deploys all aspects of social media – including diplomats using Twitter – to spread its messages and engage with a global public. It will continue to invest in infrastructure, through its 21st Century Statecraft programme, that facilitates its policy of 'complementing traditional foreign policy tools with newly innovated and adapted instruments of statecraft that fully leverage the networks, technologies, and demographics of our interconnected world'.[39] What remains to be seen is whether America's national self-interest will continue to coincide with a commitment to promoting the open Internet and whether that extends to protecting critical voices such as WikiLeaks.

In theory, the commercial companies that largely provide the infrastructure for the Internet – the cables, servers, ISPs, platforms, networks and channels such as email – also have

an interest in a relatively open Internet. The easier the connectivity, the more likely they are to reach customers and to
improve access for goods and services flowing through digital marketplaces. At the same time, companies like Google,
Amazon and Facebook have had to make pragmatic compromises in the face of pressure from authoritarian regimes such
as China. They either accept a less open Internet in those
spaces or they remove themselves from them. Either way,
freedom is compromised. However, there is a larger danger
that Timothy Wu has set out in *Master Switch*:[40] of a trend
towards consolidation of new media technologies into less
open systems. One main aspect of this he describes as the
'Kronos Effect', as larger companies eat up smaller competitors or new market entrants. Wu shows historically how
this distortion of new media markets has benefits for society
in promoting long-term investment, universal services and
robust producers. However, it also militates against innovation and competitive efficiency. Crucially, in the field of
journalism, it could reduce plurality and open access to the
public sphere for critical voices like WikiLeaks. Wu suggests
that this matters more today because 'the information indus-
tries are collectively embedded in our existence in a way
unprecedented in industrial history, involving every dimension of our national and personal lives – economic, yes, but
also expressive and cultural, social and political'.[41] He warns
that the openness of the Internet is not immutable:

> The Internet inaugurated a principle so fundamental and
> powerful that it cannot be abolished; ever after, all will
> agree that open beats closed. It is an attractive notion;
> but in fact it is an article of faith in a domain of experi-
> ence where fact, not faith, should guide us. It is true that
> the Internet naturally harnesses the power of dentralization
> and defies central control, but in the face of a determined

power, that design alone is no adequate defense of what we hold most dear about the network.[42]

WikiLeaks circumvented the problem of control by finding other servers and different payment systems. However, as we become more dependent on 'cloud computing', general freedom of speech becomes more reliant on the corporate-controlled infrastructure. Instead of storing our personal or our organization's data on our own servers, the idea of cloud computing is that we will, in effect, hire space on the web provided by commercial companies' servers. It is a very effective way to increase computational power and storage for individuals but it does mean that, technically, you have less control over your information. WikiLeaks could not have operated a 'cloud' controlled by Amazon or PayPal. Open Internet campaigners fear that we are increasingly dependent on privately owned communication spaces of democratic discourse and that private companies will not uphold wider constitutional safeguards to protect them:

> While Amazon was within its legal rights, the company has nonetheless sent a clear signal to its users: If you engage in controversial speech that some individual members of the U.S. government don't like – even if there is a strong case to be made that your speech is constitutionally protected – Amazon is going to dump you at the first sign of trouble. Let's hope that there will always be other companies willing to stand up for our rights as enshrined both in the U.S. Constitution and in the Universal Declaration of Human Rights – and by extension their right to do business with us.[43]

Despite the action taken against it in 2010, WikiLeaks was able to publish. The organizations who worked with it to publish were also untouched. However, other organizations may not wish to take the risk of alienating media corporations that provide the channels and infrastructure for transmission and funding. This hostility to dissent may not be omnipotent but it could have a 'chilling' effect. The fear is that, in the future, if a few media corporations become more dominant, then that restrictive effect might increase regardless of governmental legislation or regulation. At present, only a few companies such as Google are prepared to have this debate about their responsibilities in a relatively open and accountable fashion. However, there is no obligation upon them to do so beyond the pressure that the public – their consumers – puts upon them.

There are states, of course, that do not have the constitutional safeguards for freedom of speech enjoyed by Americans. The governments of countries like China do not want an open Internet at all. Indeed, various authoritarian regimes have tried to control, filter and even turn it off. While the Internet is a dramatic extension of the ability to communicate for individuals and networks, it also offers tools for authoritarian regimes to exert power and restrict dissent. As Evgeny Morozov has shown,[44] this is more than the denial of access to the Internet. Repressive regimes such as Iran used the connectivity of social networks and digital communications to identify, track and pursue critical voices. Morozov points out that the Internet and social networks put more traceable information online about citizens than ever before. This allows intelligence agencies to track conversations, monitor debates and intercept organizational communications. In addition, authoritarian regimes are increasingly capable of generating online propaganda with their own bloggers, websites and social networks. Those regimes can also close online platforms, block selected messages and slow down undesired traffic. *In extremis*, they can, like Mubarak in Egypt, actually 'turn off' the Internet itself.

Beyond this, Morozov goes on to question more generally how the Internet and digital communications may fail to generate a counter-culture of any real potency:

> It seems highly naive to assume that political ideas – let alone dissent – will somehow emerge from this great hodgepodge of consumerism, entertainment, and sex. As tempting as it is to think of Internet-based swinger clubs that have popped up in China in the last few years as some kind of alternative civil-society, it's quite possible that ... the Chinese Communist Party would find the space to accommodate such practices. Under the pressure of globalization, authoritarianism has become extremely accommodating.[45]

Morozov argues that, on balance, the case for the open Internet as a force for liberation has not yet been made when the negative effects are taken into account:

> If it turns out that the Internet does help to stifle dissent, amplify existing inequalities in terms of access to the media, undermine representative democracy, promote mob mentality, erode privacy, and make us less informed, it is not at all obvious how exactly the promotion of so-called Internet freedom is also supposed to assist in the promotion of democracy. Of course, it may also be true that the Internet does none of those things; the important thing is to acknowledge that the debate about the Internet's effects on democracy isn't over and to avoid behaving as if the jury is already out.[46]

The jury may not even be out, but evidence in support of the case piled up in the winter of 2010 and the spring of

2011. Morozov's book *Net Delusion* came out too early to
deal with the WikiLeaks revelations of late 2010 and 2011.
Its sceptical take on Internet democracy also appeared just
before the Arab uprisings in Tunisia and Egypt. Both those
events provide empirical evidence that further possibilities
for enhanced democratic communications are being opened
up by the Internet wherever the Internet becomes more
open. Even 'traditional' journalists say the evidence is now
'irrefutable' that social media had a significant role in those
popular rebellions:

> Facebook and other digital networks can speed political
> communication and provide efficient tools for organizing
> protests. In combination with satellite broadcasters such
> as al-Jazeera, online networks can document government
> abuses quickly and spread awareness of them. Even more,
> the promises of free speech, modernization, generational
> change, and global inclusion that these media offer – their
> very newness, and the way they connect people and ideas
> across borders – may also foster an incipient form of politi-
> cal identity for some in the fed-up urban classes in Arab
> societies and Iran.[47]

Coll is a hard-nosed foreign policy analyst, so that judgement does not spring from cyber-utopianism. However,
as the euphoria of early 2011 turned into a longer, hotter
summer where the reforms slowed down and further domi-
noes did not fall, it became clearer that the Internet is a
remarkable tool, but still only a tool. Politically, it is both
limited and ambivalent. Interestingly, the idea that the
Internet can challenge individual and journalistic freedom
as much as it supports it is one echoed by Julian Assange
himself. In a March 2011 talk to students at Cambridge
University in the UK, Assange said:

While the internet has in some ways an ability to let us know to an unprecedented level what government is doing, and to let us co-operate with each other to hold repressive governments and repressive corporations to account, it is also the greatest spying machine the world has ever seen. It [the web] is not a technology that favours freedom of speech. It is not a technology that favours human rights. It is not a technology that favours civil life. Rather it is a technology that can be used to set up a totalitarian spying regime, the likes of which we have never seen. Or, on the other hand, taken by us, taken by activists, and taken by all those who want a different trajectory for the technological world, it can be something we all hope for.[48]

Despite his accomplishments relying on technologies only made possible thanks to the Internet and its infrastructure, Assange and other WikiLeaks supporters recognize the technology is in a period of transition, during which its consequences for open information, activism and reporting are still far from clear. Much more evidence is needed on the political impacts of this cycle of new technological development. We will discuss the wider relevance of the media and the Arab Spring in chapter 4, but in itself the latter cannot be a confirmation of the progressive political power of the open Internet. Media effects are notoriously difficult to quantify, and causality is especially hard to define. So it makes more sense to focus attention on the dynamics and ethics of policy-making in relation to media, and on an analysis of how information flows are being reconfigured, rather than attempting to reach any firm conclusions about the intrinsic nature of the Internet. It is vital to heed Morozov's warning that a naïve faith in the automatically democratic nature of the Internet can lead to policy mistakes by governments and other agencies seeking to promote liberal ideas.

Excessive technological determinism can mean opportunities are missed to foster or protect the democratic opportunities of the Internet. Morozov advocates a 'cyber-realism' that seeks to promote locally relevant and sustainable initiatives.

We will look at those possible initiatives in more detail in the following parts of this chapter, but if WikiLeaks is part of opening up the Internet, then how effective has it been in closed societies? Is WikiLeaks a vehicle for driving the open Internet agenda into currently restricted parts of cyberspace? Despite its earlier claim to be targeting China, WikiLeaks has not been able to obtain leaks from states that adopt more authoritarian controls over their information security and a tighter management of their mainstream and private social media. As we see in the following section on WikiLeaks as a model, there is no 'ChinaLeaks' (except in the realms of satire[49]). Clearly, in authoritarian states, Assange cannot collaborate with independent mainstream media partners to amplify the revelations. It is difficult to measure to what degree the WikiLeaks cable revelations about these countries reached the publics concerned. Certainly, state-owned and mass media outlets ignored anything critical of their ruling elites. There is some evidence that WikiLeaks did have an impact in the Tunisian revolution. The WikiLeaks cable in which American diplomats confirmed allegations of corruption by President Ben Ali were quoted by activists.[50] In that sense, Gideon Rachman of the *Financial Times* is right when he suggests that WikiLeaks might actually be a positive development for American foreign policy as it attempts to expose repressive regimes to the wider world and their own people. Rachman points out that generally the cables show that America is acting in private according to the liberal values it expresses in public:

There have been a few revelations that do not reflect well on the Americans. There is the order to US diplomats at the United Nations to hoover up personal details of UN officials, including credit card numbers. . . . Overall, the picture of the US that emerges from WikiLeaks is positive. America's foreign policy comes across as principled, intelligent and pragmatic. That was, perhaps, the best-kept secret of all.[51]

Inevitably, the debate around the cables was constructed in relation to America because that is where they came from. However, the real impact has been on countries such as Saudi Arabia, where the information they contained was not part of the public political sphere. Even in a closed state like Saudi, the Internet means that some people will now have become aware of the degree of their rulers' hostility to Iran and their enjoyment of rather risqué parties.[52] What we do not know is the effect that the very act of the release will have as an instructive example of the power of unauthorized information release.

Julian Assange still thinks that WikiLeaks will have impact on closed societies as well as open liberal states, and that ultimately China is a better target. This is not because it is more likely to respond in a liberalizing way regarding information or the Internet. Instead, he argues that the commercialization of democracy in America means that they have traded radical politics for material comfort. Other societies are still fundamentally political, according to Assange, and therefore open to real change:

we believe it is the most closed societies that have the most reform potential. The Chinese case is quite interesting. Aspects of the Chinese government, Chinese Public Security Service, appear to be terrified of free speech, and while one might say that means something awful is happening in the country, I actually think that is a very optimistic sign, because it means that speech can still cause reform and that the power structure is still inherently political, as opposed to fiscal. So journalism and writing are capable of achieving change, and that is why Chinese authorities are so scared of it. Whereas in the United States to a large degree, and in other Western countries, the basic elements of society have been so heavily fiscalized through contractual obligations that political change doesn't seem to result in economic change, which in other words means that political change doesn't result in change.[53]

That argument feels rather hopeful and not a little convoluted. It is typical of the unusual world-view that Assange has evolved. Neither does it explain how WikiLeaks is going to have an impact in China in practice. For there to be a political effect it still requires acts of 'journalism and writing' that challenge power. In the digital era, those acts depend on something that Hillary Clinton and Julian Assange agree with. This is the idea that the open Internet will ultimately strengthen open states while those that restrict digital networks will weaken their economic as well as their political power. The hope is that political communications will be able to swim in the same digital channels as the commercial or social streams. One of the key insights of Assange was that, strategically, he was forcing his targets to make a choice about how they related to the Internet:

If their behavior is revealed to the public, they have one of two choices: one is to reform in such a way that they can be proud of their endeavors, and proud to display them to the public. Or the other is to lock down internally and to Balkanize, and as a result, of course, cease to be as efficient as they were. To me, that is a very good outcome, because organizations can either be efficient, open and honest, or they can be closed, conspiratorial and inefficient.[54]

So far, in China's case at least, this has been a sacrifice that the ruling classes have been prepared to make. Their economy does not appear to be collapsing within the Great Firewall. Indeed, they are globalizing their economic and political strength while maintaining internal 'harmony'. It may be that freedom of expression campaigner John Kampfner is closer to the truth with his argument that citizens in states like China are more likely to accept minimal reform around issues such as freedom of expression in exchange for material and social security.[55] This is a view consistent with the presence of a large and well-educated middle class in China, many of whom are able to travel outside of the country and can hardly be said to be ignorant of the outside world. This middle class is potentially the only one an organization such as WikiLeaks could hope to reach. At the moment it seems to prioritize stability and strong economic growth over democratic reform.

Kampfner also warns that criticism of WikiLeaks in America and the attempts to undermine its infrastructure and prosecute Assange will embolden authoritarian regimes in their actions to restrict media freedom:

> The hysterical response of many to the WikiLeaks controversy, particularly in the US . . . has played into the hands of the Kremlin, the Chinese Communist party, Robert Mugabe, Burma's generals and other assorted dictators around the world. Every time now a dissident, activist or blogger is arrested, regimes such as these can wave two fingers at international concern. 'You did it, so why can't we?' will come the response.[56]

So, in the battle for an open Internet, it is clear that WikiLeaks occupies a complex position. It survives relatively unscathed because of the structural freedom of the Internet. Yet it is unable to gather or disseminate material in the societies where the Internet is more controlled. The impact of its revelations where they concern those states rarely has a sustained political effect. While there is evidence for the liberating power of the Internet in some places over certain periods, there is still no clear sense of the ability of WikiLeaks to play a significant role in those states where it is unable to network into mainstream media. In open systems effectively run by private industry, there is also the danger that corporations seeking market dominance will degrade net neutrality in a way that affects content as well as traffic. WikiLeaks is dependent on the open Internet for its survival, but that alone does not guarantee it will have the impact that it was created to achieve.

## 3.3 WIKILEAKS AS A MODEL

'Courage is contagious', that is, when someone engages in a courageous act and shows other people that that act wasn't an act of martyrdom, rather that it was an intelligently designed act, it encourages other people to follow him.[57]

If WikiLeaks works, then why are there not more of them? Large numbers of people think that Julian Assange is personally brave and politically inspiring. WikiLeaks has attracted widespread support, including fund-raising, hospitality and other forms of active help. However, comparable organizations, or further leaks on the same scale, have not emerged in its immediate wake. Not yet, at least. It may simply be a matter of time. The other possibility is that WikiLeaks was an exception or one-off. By examining the future of

WikiLeaks as a media model, we can understand its significance but also explore the potential evolution of journalism
in the mature Internet age. Is it a model for others? 'The
fundamental issues surrounding WikiLeaks are not the over-
blown claims about transparency made by its founder, but
the questions of whether the model of the electronic drop
box – and protection of sources by software code rather than
ethical code – are robust and replicable by others.'[58]

WikiLeaks has already spawned clones and other versions
that deploy similar whistle-blowing data techniques. All
have in common the desire to benefit from the fundamental
exceptionalism of WikiLeaks: that it has removed itself from
conventional media's dependency on a geographical location and a national legal framework. Although many adopt
the -Leaks suffix they do vary in their legal status, aims and
methods.

Some of the clones have a very niche area, such as
JumboLeaks[59] based at Tufts University that appears to
be a way of holding the university to account on issues
like endowments. Some, like ThaiLeaks,[60] appear to provide a mirror site for published WikiLeaks documents for
countries in which the original site is blocked. Others, like
GlobalLeaks,[61] are seeking to create a distributed network
of secure platforms on the WikiLeaks model, but without
taking responsibility for the publication of the information
– instead, it would be handed over to journalists. At the time
of writing it was still evolving its modus operandi. Some versions have already received the compliment of denunciation
and reprisals from governments. JamiiForums[62] in Tanzania
has provided a popular platform for leaks and anonymous
comment. It has been attacked by ministers and bombarded
with hostile pro-government postings.[63] None of these sites
had much in the way of sustained or widespread impact by
mid-2011.

This may be simply a question of building momentum. They lack WikiLeaks' first-mover advantage, although many benefit from having a more specific focus. They may also have technical problems, especially around security. It may also be that the big-scale data dump disclosure is much harder to achieve – especially of meaningful information – than was thought. Without hacking it relies on deliberate – usually criminal – insider disclosure. As we have said, that is a very old-fashioned journalistic act that may depend on chance. Bradley Manning may have been an unusual person in a rare position. Perhaps what is remarkable about modern data systems, with the vast flows of information and the thousands of people involved in processing the data, is how rarely they are breached. This may be why, for example, the BrusselsLeaks website is so modest in its claims and, at the time of writing, so slow to publish anything: 'This is a place to get the truth out. Brussels is by no means a sexy place and we want to control expectations. Many documents might be technical and might, at the time, not seem totally relevant. But they document something very important – they document how decisions are arrived at and where future policy might go.'[64]

As we saw in chapter 1, WikiLeaks had many leaks before Bradley Manning's alleged disclosures, but none achieved the volume of that material. The second problem is the dissemination of those leaks. Assange needed the partnership with mainstream media to process the information into a format that worked on platforms with ready-made mass audiences. That worked in the West and in democratic states like India but not yet in intermediate societies like Russia and certainly not in closed ones like Iran or Cuba. So, inevitably, those that seek to emulate WikiLeaks may well need to reformulate both their intended audience and the nature of the information they handle. There are also some practical issues that need to be addressed. Those working in these neo-WikiLeaks operations will need better training and skills in handling data but also in risk management and secure operating procedures. The organizations will need to keep creating better donation systems, adaptable security and storage facilities.[65]

## 3.4  HACKTAVISM REDUX

Some adherents to the disruptive aims of WikiLeaks want a return to its roots in 'hacktavist' culture. The loose network of hackers called Anonymous came to WikiLeaks' aid during the 2010 attacks on its infrastructure. It launched DDOS assaults on those corporations who withdrew services from WikiLeaks with great enthusiasm, but with debatable results. An Anonymous 'member' claimed a role for the pure leaker site that can operate without the aid of mainstream media:

> I predict that Anonymous and entities like it will become far more significant over the next few years than is expected by most of our similarly irrelevant pundits – and this will, no doubt, turn out to be just as much of an understatement as anything else that has been written on the subject. The fact is that the technological infrastructure that allows these movements has been in place for well under a decade – but phenomena such as WikiLeaks and Anonymous have already appeared, expanded, and even become players within the geo-political environment; others have come about since. This is the future, whether one approves or not, and the failure on the part of governments and media alike to understand, and contend with the rapid change now afoot, ought to remind everyone concerned why it is that this movement is necessary in the first place.[66]

It is possible governments and corporations may soon hanker for the days of WikiLeaks, and recognize the relative merits of its hybrid, semi-journalistic model. Certainly, when the far more anarchic collectives Anonymous or LulzSec have obtained material, they have been far less reserved in its release than WikiLeaks was with its 2010 releases. Having obtained the internal emails of security firm HBGary, Anonymous published them in full. LulzSec managed to get account details of millions of users from a plethora of sites in its short lifespan. Both groups vowed to target the government and would likely publish material in a less censored – and therefore potentially less safe – but also less accessible way. To that extent, the groups may represent a threat to the mainstream media as well as to the organizations they target.

Perhaps the real threat of hacktavism is not to specific channels of secret government information, but to the security of systems itself. The LulzSec group's attacks on Sony, revealing customers' data, was in itself fairly innocuous and it only had a temporary existence as a network. If replicated more often, however, exploits like this might have the effect of undermining confidence in the ability of corporations to keep data safe.[67] Certainly, major organizations like NATO take the wider threat of cyber-attacks from individuals and groups, as well as hostile governments, seriously. They think hackers, rather than WikiLeaks, could not just compromise their information systems but render their military defences less secure:

> The ongoing information revolution poses a series of political, cultural, economic as well as national security challenges. Changing communications, computing and information storage patterns are challenging notions such as privacy, identity, national borders and societal structures. The profound changes inherent in this revolution are also

changing the way we look at security, often in unantici-
pated ways, and demanding innovative responses. It is said
that because of this revolution, the time it takes to cross
the Atlantic has shrunk to 30 milliseconds, compared with
30 minutes for ICBMs and several months going by boat.
Meanwhile, a whole new family of actors is emerging on
the international stage, such as virtual 'hacktavist' groups.
These could potentially lead to a new class of international
conflicts between these groups and nation states, or even to
conflicts between exclusively virtual entities.[68]

That kind of geo-political scenario scoping might over-
state the dangers. Among the problems that WikiLeak and
Anonymous face are scale and sustainability. How do you
maximize the impact of the release, and how do you continue
to leak over time? WikiLeaks attempted to solve the problem of achieving reach, impact and influence by networking
into mainstream media, something that Anonymous is only
just starting to consider.

Anonymous rose to mainstream fame – or notoriety –
after hacking the email logs of a security firm, HBGary, who
had put together proposals for Bank of America on how to
neutralize WikiLeaks. The leaderless organization, and its
offshoot LulzSec, were more cavalier than WikiLeaks in
both how they obtained and how they published information: information was grabbed directly through hacking, and
disseminated in full, often through peer-to-peer networks.
Yet by the summer of 2011, even Anonymous was reconsid-
ering. Having claimed to have obtained 4 GB from the UK's
*Sun* newspaper, Anonymous decided against publishing –
saying instead it would be working with media organizations
to disseminate any useful information, to avoid the risk of
jeopordizing legal cases in ongoing phone hacking prosecu-
tions of several former News Corporation employees.

At the time of writing, such collaborations were yet to materialize, in part due to a string of arrests of alleged senior members of Anonymous and LulzSec – but the collectives' decision to mirror the WikiLeaks model has implications for the trend of other hacking or transparency activists on the Internet.

### 3.5 ADVOCACY NGO JOURNALISM

Assange sees WikiLeaks as a revolutionary project that is a radical 'intelligence agency of the people' in the tradition of left-wing and 'grass-roots' newspapers.[69] He says that his collaboration with mainstream media is mere 'realpolitik' and that WikiLeaks' real 'base' is 'more than 50 regional publishers, activist groups and charities, giving them early access to hundreds – or in some cases, thousands – of documents relevant to their countries or causes'.[70] In practice, there is little evidence of WikiLeaks actually giving any NGOs 'early access' or having particularly close relationships with them. But why not take it farther and create a WikiLeaks that works on specific topics and with particular supporters and aims?

Charities, lobby groups and NGOs like Greenpeace or Oxfam have been professional media organizations for some decades now. They have hired journalists to create communications for their own supporters, as well as public relations material that can be used by mainstream media. New media technologies now allow them to gather information and broadcast it directly through websites and social networks. The mediation is partly for fund-raising but also for political ends. It can be effective in shaping public responses to specific crises or issues and more generally in influencing decision-makers and helping to construct mainstream media agendas.[71] Most NGOs have gone beyond mere service pro-

vision and the alleviation of suffering to a strategy where
they seek an impact on policy through political advocacy. So
that might make them an obvious candidate for collaboration
with organizations like WikiLeaks. However, NGOs are not
always entirely transparent and accountable in their use of
new communications channels.[72] NGOs use information to
promote political or policy ends, not necessarily to create a
full debate or to engage in self-criticism. Information flows,
along with transparency and accountability, tend to be in one
direction. So, while working with a WikiLeaks-type organization may give them more ammunition in their assault on
power, it may not give the public a complete picture. It may
reinforce the tendency to convert public debate into competing lobbying and marketing campaigns: 'Underlying some
NGOs' ambivalence about participating in the media may
be a deeper desire to exercise caution in exposing themselves
to critical debate about development issues in the public
sphere.'[73]

The former WikiLeaks operative Daniel Domscheit-Berg
has created OpenLeaks, a secure data drop facility on the
WikiLeaks model. He has indicated that it will work with
NGOs who will publish the information, probably in collaboration with news organizations. That would give it
structural support but arguably could be seen to compromise
its neutrality. The danger for the platform is that it would
be seen as an NGO public relations operation. Acting as an
information agency for advocacy organizations would end
the WikiLeaks model's claim to be an open platform for
whistle-blowers. If its revelations were directly connected
to a cause, then the more general credibility it enjoys as a
disruptive platform would be replaced with a much more
functional, propagandist position. WikiLeaks made no pre-
tence of neutrality over its leaks concerning, for example, the
Iraq or Afghan wars. But if it is selecting leaks and fashioning

specific relationships with lobby groups, inevitably it weakens its own claim to independence and therefore, perhaps, to public trust. Conversely, for the NGO there would be the risk of a loss of control over the message and the danger that the act of whistle-blowing would put it into legally and editorially controversial areas. Some NGOs, such as Greenpeace, trade on that kind of frisson, but others might find it too risky a strategy.

## 3.6 FOUNDATION AND PUBLIC JOURNALISM

We have seen how OpenLeaks aims to team up with NGOs, but, increasingly, investigative and challenging journalism is turning itself into civil society organizations. In the past, investigative journalism was part of the wider news media institution. The famous Insight team at the British *Sunday Times* newspaper is the classic example. Its reputation may have been somewhat mythologized thanks to the pioneering investigation into the Thalidomide drug scandal, but it remains a benchmark for an investigative journalism strategy.[74] The Insight team was a group of journalists dedicated to longer-term, in-depth and revelatory investigations. Set up in 1963, it was a kind of elite specialist unit, but still financially and editorially part of the wider newspaper. It was financed by the same sales and advertising and it could reach an audience who turned to the paper for its more general news, features and sport. This mixed model of cross-subsidization and cross-fertilization is under threat because of the economic crisis in mainstream media.[75] Paul Starr's warning about American newspapers resonates across any mainstream media engaged in the more expensive task of revelatory and challenging journalism in a time of crisis for the Western journalism business model: 'More than any other medium, newspapers have been our eyes on the state, our check on private abuses, our civic alarm systems. It is true that they have often failed to perform those functions as well as they should have done. But whether they can continue to perform them at all is now in doubt.'[76]

As resources for dedicated investigative and political journalism are reduced, there have been attempts to fund it directly from external sources by creating separate institutions. These are usually non-profit and depend on direct philanthropy for core funding and so have been labelled 'Foundation Journalism'.

Just when mainstream journalism becomes faster and shallower, this subsidized mode of production offers the potential of deeper, more reflective and researched journalism. Investigative journalism is finding new ways to support itself that allow it to do different things. In America there is very little journalism funded directly by local or national government. There is, however, a culture of philanthropic funding for foundations that promote public-service journalism. Increasingly, these have sought to provide funds directly to community and investigative journalism units outside of mainstream media newsrooms. Examples include Propublica, the Huffington Post Investigative Fund, Spot.us and a Knight Foundation-funded multimedia project at the Center for Investigative Reporting. They adopt novel production processes to varying degrees, but they see themselves as a way of correcting a market failure and encouraging editorial innovation rather than challenging 'quality' mainstream media in their role in holding power to account: 'Though these ventures seek, like WikiLeaks, to use new technologies to transform the way in which investigative work is produced and distributed, they are firmly committed to traditional journalistic values and see themselves as preserving an industry at least as much as reshaping it.'[77]

WikiLeaks itself originally sought funding from similar

sources but the fact that it exists outside of national boundaries and does not have a clear internal governance structure
makes it difficult for it to meet the administrative conditions
that govern that kind of resourcing. For the same reasons,
it would be difficult for foundation journalism to provide
the immunity WikiLeaks enjoys. That does not mean that
the two types cannot collaborate – however, they may suffer
similar tensions to those between WikiLeaks and mainstream media. As we have seen, the foundation-funded
British Bureau of Investigative Journalism struggled to cope
with the demands of working with WikiLeaks and its mainstream media collaborators.

These new forms of foundation journalism may re-
animate the debate around the American idea of 'Public
Journalism' that arose in the 1990s. This was the journalistic
movement that sought to foreground the ethical impact as
well as professional coda of the news media. It stressed the
responsibility of journalism to foster citizen engagement in
public debate. As one of those involved in implementing the
theory at the time has recently written, the new technologies
that facilitate networked journalism offer fresh potential for
the ideas of public journalism: 'Citizen-generated journalism based on public journalism principles can help both our
public life and the press go well, but only through deliberate,
dedicated effort.'[78]

So advocates of public journalism in the digital age hope
that increased public participation in a more networked
journalism can rejuvenate the role of the news media as
public sphere: 'As a democratic midwife, the Fourth Estate
can re-assume the role that has been eroded away by public
cynicism about politicians and the political process, and the
media's links to both.'[79]

This is still predicated on John Dewey's idea that journalism's job is to keep public opinion informed and to

foster debate.[80] It is a fairly general ideal and impossible to realize in any complete sense. It is an aspiration as well as an applied function for journalism. Yet, this moderately reformist ambition is in keeping with Julian Assange's conception of WikiLeaks' purpose as part of a healthy democracy: 'WikiLeaks is part of an honourable tradition that expands the scope of freedom by trying to lay "all the mysteries and secrets of government" before the public.'[81]

So, foundation funding combined with public participation would appear to offer a non-market-based ethical new business model for journalism:

> The ability of more traditionally organized nonprofits to leverage their capabilities in an environment where the costs of doing business are sufficiently lower than they were in the print and television era that they can sustain effective newsrooms staffed with people who, like academic faculties, are willing to sacrifice some of the bottom line in exchange for the freedom to pursue their professional values.[82]

There are practical problems. Foundation journalism is dependent upon philanthropic institutions or public generosity. Both are limited and unpredictable. National Public Radio (NPR) in America has shown that those sources of income are sustainable but difficult to grow to any significant scale. Public participation adds value but it still requires curation. Organizations like Propublica still rely upon mainstream media to provide a wider platform to disseminate (and part-fund) their work. There is also the problem that these media organizations can be influenced by the agenda of their funders. A combination of high ethics standards, a desire for high quality, and large editorial boards can occasionally make such foundations more cautious than mainstream media organizations. Their discrete nature may also mean that they are cut off from wider flows of information and interaction. Much investigative journalism, for example, flows from general news coverage rather than arising separately. Foundation and citizen journalism projects benefit from their removal from mainstream pressure to produce routine news, but they may cut themselves off from the wider context which public journalism must include.

Foundation journalists we have spoken to worry that mainstream media organizations see them as a way of getting quality journalism at a discount. Their work is a subsidy rather than a bold expansion of what mainstream media do. At the same time most of them have to raise extra funds as part of the condition of their foundation funding so they are compelled to deal with the commercial news organizations. That also means that the editorial product has to conform to the expectations of the commercial editors. This is not a recipe for ground-breaking or disruptive journalism. However, foundation news production can offer greater editorial diversity than mainstream media in their increasingly constrained state. It can cover subjects that are not so popular and it can do it in a way that is less sensational. It can also focus on particular aspects, such as investigative journalism, rather than overall coverage. However, generally, foundation journalism still cleaves to the aspiration of objective journalism. It is not as radically risk-taking as WikiLeaks, because it is seeking institutional sustainability. It is more responsible than WikiLeaks because it is held to account by its funders. In some ways, it is also more responsible than much of commercial mainstream media because it is often beholden to an overtly ethical code or mission statement established by the foundation funding. However, it is still insider not outsider journalism that seeks to reform and enhance existing political and media structures, not change them.

## 3.7  MAINSTREAM WHISTLE-BLOWERS

By their very nature, mainstream media organizations cannot replicate WikiLeaks as an organization. While whistle-blowing and leaking have always been part of mainstream media, they cannot have the same degree of immunity and their calculation of risk will always be significantly different (see section 1.3). Mainstream media organizations have a geographical base and are subject to national laws. They are also under commercial, funding and political pressures to operate within a consensual framework that permits limited transgressions and a relative degree of oppositional discourse. However, some mainstream organizations are using the same technologies as WikiLeaks, such as encryption and anonymized communication, to create similar projects within their more general news production.

The Al Jazeera Transparency Unit, for example, achieved a massive release of confidential data with its publication of the so-called 'Palestine Papers'. In the area of Middle East geo-politics, that story arguably had as great an impact on current politics as anything published by WikiLeaks.[83] These comprised 'nearly 1,700 files, thousands of pages of diplomatic correspondence detailing the inner workings of the Israeli–Palestinian peace process ... memos, e-mails, maps, minutes from private meetings, accounts of high level exchanges, strategy papers and even power point presentations ... from 1999 to 2010'.[84]

The papers were presented in the same way as the *New York Times* and the *Guardian* published the WikiLeaks cables, with selected highlights, original documents and commentary all provided on the website. The Unit promises leakers the same anonymity and security as WikiLeaks and to an extent it enjoys a degree of immunity itself.

Al Jazeera's structure of funding and organization gives it

a remarkable degree of freedom to pursue critical journalism around the world. It is very well resourced, as a TV channel (or two channels) but also as a powerful online presence with a wide range of social media platforms and projects. Its funding from the ruler of the rich but tiny Gulf state Qatar precludes criticism of the Emir but also appears to some critics to coincide with a wider editorial bias.[85] Al Jazeera has been accused of not pursuing its enthusiastic coverage of the Arab uprisings when they threatened other Gulf states on good terms with Qatar. Indeed, material contained within WikiLeaks' own editorial cache shows Qatari politicians have not hesitated in using Al Jazeera as a bargaining chip in international negotiations.[86] But that funding also means that, more generally, it does not have to worry about commercial or political pressure from the subjects of its work. So in that sense it is protected to a similar degree to an independent licence-fee-funded organization like the BBC, but with the ability to take editorial gambles such as the Palestine Papers and to pursue more 'campaigning' revelatory journalism. The Transparency Unit still retains editorial control for itself and Al Jazeera. Submissions of video, documents or simply tip-offs can be made securely but the journalists will control the verification and publication process. This is more of an advanced citizen journalism news-gathering exercise than an open whistle-blowing platform.

Newspapers do not get much more mainstream than the *Wall Street Journal*, owned by Rupert Murdoch and a bastion of quality international financial and business journalism. It has now set up SafeHouse,[87] which provides a secure facility for leakers to release documents and information. However, it is not clear how different this is from the traditional function of newspapers as recipients of leaks. The stand-alone site will have its own servers, but in its terms and conditions it warns leakers that the *Journal* reserves various rights, such as to disclose information about the leaker as well as the leak to the authorities. It also says that it will not break the law: 'If we enter into a confidential relationship, Dow Jones will take all available measures to protect your identity while remaining in compliance with all applicable laws.'

SafeHouse may well end up as a drop box for some intriguing documents, but it is not conceived as, and will not be, a challenge to power. The idea of a Rupert Murdoch-owned newspaper, however independent it might be, actually challenging the status quo seems unlikely. So it seems that mainstream media will be able to do more to facilitate leakers but they will remain within the traditional framework of the rights and responsibilities that apply in the rest of their coverage. As we shall see in the final chapter, there may well be a future for WikiLeaks and its variants, but in a networked world there are a plethora of other potential channels for critiquing authority.

# 4

## SOCIAL MEDIA AS DISRUPTIVE JOURNALISM: MEDIA, POLITICS AND NETWORK EFFECTS

In this chapter, we will look at WikiLeaks in relation to how wider social media are producing new kinds of political communications that are performing comparable functions to WikiLeaks. The role, for example, of social media in the Arab Spring of 2011 suggests that new forms of disruptive and challenging communication are emerging in social networks online and on mobile phones. We will go back to WikiLeaks in particular as an organization and ask how it might survive or disappear. Can it simply continue in its current form, or will it have to adapt to a more sustainable structure? And if it does change, how will it evolve? Finally, we will discuss WikiLeaks as a network exploit; how WikiLeaks has created a hybrid position as a networked journalism organization that retains characteristics of alternative media. What significance does this have for political journalism in a world where power is networked? How is journalism and the idea of news itself changing in the WikiLeaks world?

## 4.1 TRANSPARENCY AND THE NETWORK

WikiLeaks is part of the widespread network of information flows on the Internet. It has gained extraordinary reach across languages and states. In this it has benefited from its collaboration with numerous mainstream media online platforms that have packaged and presented the material to their own readership communities – these in turn are linked on to aggregator sites and through social media referrals. WikiLeaks has also gained widespread publicity through broadcast and other media covering WikiLeaks as a story in itself, thanks partly to the attention focused on Julian Assange and partly to the political drama around WikiLeaks as security threat and an affront to mainstream media values. It has also benefited from enthusiastic promotion and citation by individual citizens, as well as campaigning groups like Avaaz. At the time of writing, Avaaz's online petition to 'Stop the Crackdown' on WikiLeaks had been signed by 750,000 people.[1] WikiLeaks is seen as a cause as well as a media organization. The main way to support it – apart from donations – is to share the information it reveals through links across email, websites and social networks like Twitter and Facebook. It is a good example of the new networked effects of the Internet on the dissemination of journalism. The online public does more than simply consume news. Readers exponentially amplify the distribution of stories in a highly efficient way, because generally they will be connected to people who will tend to share their interests and pass on material to their networks in turn. So readers act as publisher, filter, gatekeeper, and curator of news. They will sometimes re-version, adapt or dissect that news. In addition, they might comment, critique or analyse that information. They can also reverse the flow and interact back to the orginator – in this case, WikiLeaks. So it is not surprising that cyber-optimists see WikiLeaks as the precursor of a new age in which that kind of revelatory networked media is abundant:

> An old way of doing things is dying; a new one is being born ... Old institutions and incumbent powers are inexorably coming to terms with this new reality. The "Age of Transparency" is here: not because one transnational online network dedicated to open information and whistle-blowing named WikiLeaks exists, but because the knowledge of how to build and maintain such networks is now widespread.[2]

As we consider the significance of WikiLeaks for the future of journalism, perhaps we should not be treating it simply as a replicable model or a template. It might be that the WikiLeaks potential could be fully realized, not in its particular organizational form, but in the networks inhabited by the information it reproduces. Can wider, political social media themselves have similar effects to WikiLeaks? Can they produce challenging, revelatory 'journalism' that promotes real transparency and accountability to power? Certainly, digitally enabled 'citizens as journalists' can supplement and transform journalism through networked public participation: 'A distributed population armed with cameras and video recorders and a distributed population of experts and insiders who can bring more expertise and direct experience to bear on the substance of any given story will provide tremendous benefits of quality, depth, and context to any story.'[3]

Is it possible that the networked journalism on social networks can operate without (or alongside) mainstream media infrastructure in a critical, disruptive way? Can it constitute a more continual and autonomous process of accountability? Will transparency become ingrained in our personal networked relationships with each other and with the sources or holders of information? In other words, will we secure more transparency through Twitter? Again, some cyber-optimists are convinced that a kind of networked collective can deliver this: 'In a digitized and networked world, Zuckerberg, Assange, and their outfits are merely avatars of the inexorable march toward a radically greater degree of transparency in our personal, cultural, and political spheres. The question about the new transparency isn't how to thwart it – because we can't. The question is how we live with it.'[4]

Putting the founders of Facebook and WikiLeaks together as 'avatars' of an onward march towards transparency highlights the ambiguity of the idea, as Heilemann intended in that quote. While Assange is assaulting the right of states to retain information, Zuckerberg is challenging our notions and control of personal privacy. But both presume that there should be and will be greater openness or disclosure. What if that transparency really was complete? What if the example of WikiLeaks led to a truly open public sphere? John Lloyd is a journalist and researcher who is currently writing a report on the idea of transparency.[5] He has been sceptical of the claims made for citizen participation and social media as forces for improved accountability journalism. However, he accepts it is theoretically possible that we could have a world where everything was potentially transparent:

We – and especially our leaders – would develop into super-rational beings uncomprehending of the notion of mendacity. Politicians would give the whole range of their thoughts on every subject, in support of their party or otherwise; officials would make public their plans at every stage; diplomats would reveal all conversations and the public would have the maturity to understand and take no unfair advantage of these disclosures.[6]

Unfortunately, as John Lloyd goes on to say, this idyllic state is impractical and politically against the odds: 'No conceivable society could live in such transparency. It is more likely that a transparency culture simply causes a displacement of the semi-private into the wholly private – with public figures relying more on public relations to act as a shield, and turning an increasingly bland face to the outside word.'[7]

So total transparency may be both impossible and undesirable. However, it is clear that the status quo is not an option, mainly because public expectations about information have changed: 'The notion of a 30-year rule in which patrician officials deign to allow us, long after the protagonists have left the scene, knowledge of what was done in our name, is surely over. Policy making has been demystified.'[8]

So we are about to enter a phase in which authorities negotiate a new balance and system of information accountability, and that means, in effect, a new relationship between the citizen, information and the state. Governments across the world have put far more data into the public domain. They will also argue that much of their workings must remain confidential. It is not just diplomacy that demands some degree of secrecy. If all policy-making and executive processes are exposed to total transparency, then decision-making would become inhibited and a culture of no risk taking and no debate might ensue. So can governments act to stem the shift to transparency? Yes, additional laws, regulations or physical limits that restrain the flow of information in social networks and on the rest of the Internet are possible. However, to a degree, the expense in terms of administrating these controls would be prohibitive. The US diplomatic cables that WikiLeaks leaked were part of a move after 9/11 to greater information sharing amongst the State Department and its outlying embassies and other agencies. More effective and efficient government was predicated upon greater flows of information and that made it vulnerable to some data escaping the system. But while there have been changes to the amount or type of information that is now exchanged in that system and who has access, the fundamental policy needs mean that the scale of communications will continue.

So the key question is not whether there is a process underway of reconfiguring information flows, but whether it will evolve into a new political information paradigm:

> We have more knowledge, but are we able to, do we have time to, indeed do we really want to act on it? Will our security services now act any differently? Are our banks acting any differently? Once they have sorted out their online filtering system, will our diplomats and governments act any differently? Everything has changed and nothing has changed.[9]

## 4.2 SOCIAL MEDIA AS POLITICAL COMMUNICATIONS: 'THE ARAB SPRING'

To understand how the shift of power might happen, it is useful to look at an exceptional and unpredicted case. If we look in more detail at the recent uprisings in the Arab world, it is possible to see how the political use of different new media is 'changing things'. WikiLeaks has a part to play in this process, but this latest phase of disruptive media innovation is more complex than any particular actors or platforms.

In December 2010, Google's Executive Chairman Eric Schmidt and Director of Ideas Jared Cohen wrote a lengthy optimistic outline of a more accountable future shaped by the Internet: 'The advent and power of connection technologies – tools that connect people to vast amounts of information and to one another – will make the twenty-first century all about surprises. Governments will be caught off-guard when large numbers of their citizens, armed with virtually nothing but cell phones, take part in mini-rebellions that challenge their authority.'[10]

Within a month, the 'mini-rebellions' they prophesied were surprisingly big. Social media did not 'cause' the revolutions in Tunisia or Egypt. However, if one wanted to find out where the next uprising in the Middle East might occur, then social media are now useful indicators, if not predictors, of political change. Regardless of the specifics of the causal relationship, social media do seem to be a critical factor in the evolution of a more networked kind of politics. This politics may not be defined by an overarching ideology or aim, but it does seem to have an element of what Schmidt and Cohen called 'surprise' and what we could also call 'uncertainty'.

The most important pre-conditions for revolution are economic. Both Tunisia and Egypt had recently suffered downturns after periods when their economies had become relatively developed. However, that growth was characterized by severe income inequality and corruption that meant the rewards were unevenly and perversely distributed and safeguards were not established. The politics is also vital. Both countries were ruled by repressive, rigid and kleptocratic regimes. The safety valves for dissent or protest were blocked, with mainstream media largely state-owned or state-controlled. Military, police and intelligence agencies were in the service of the governments in the effort to suppress dissent and restrict freedoms. In both states the machine for maintaining power and resisting change was becoming sclerotic.

Then there were other structural social factors. Demography created a surplus of dispossessed and unengaged youth with much better education but little to gain from it. There was a middle class who felt under-appreciated by the regime and over-burdened fiscally. There was a commercial sector that was simultaneously constricted by bureaucracy and exploited by corruption. Rising levels of education and contact with the wider world created populations that were more aware of alternatives and the techniques for organization. These factors played into historic grievances and an aspiration to revive national ideals.

All these factors drove revolutions in Tunisia and Egypt and have fuelled uprisings elsewhere in the Arab world. They may also do so in other regions. But in an increasingly mediated world, communications become more important as tools and catalysts. New media technologies are a key and growing part of this, but they have to be seen in the wider context of mass media such as radio or TV. Increasingly, that communications context spreads across borders, thanks to the Internet and satellite TV. It is difficult to explain how Egypt caught fire without noting how many people there made a direct link to the Tunisian example seen online and on TV.

The testimony of those involved and the evidence that is now emerging as we understand the sequencing of change is that the uprisings were crucially galvanized and facilitated by social media operating, in a networked way, with mainstream – and especially international – news media. In turn this network of communications was part of the real-world manifestations in the streets and squares that physically and symbolically represented the actual threat to power.

The role of media in these uprisings was not just instrumental. The 'networkedness' of the communications reflected and shaped the political organization. These two uprisings were not led by organized conventional opposition parties or charismatic leaders. They were not directly connected to a major event such as an election (as in Iran) or an external conflict or internal military coup. They arose incrementally and were then accelerated by a few highly symbolic individual acts combined with multiple collective connections. Some of those actions involved great heroism and suffering, even death. Generally, the initial response to them was networked and diffuse, and directed to nominal goals such as a demonstration. The organizing principle would be a date or a rallying cry honouring an individual, rather than a political slogan: 'We are all Khaled Said.'[11]

This relatively amorphous organization was connected around nodal figures that all tended to resist conventional leadership roles. The momentum was begun with plural, marginal actions such as a few silent protesters filmed for a YouTube video on a railway line with their hands on their mouths.[12]

These physical acts were communicated through social media: mobile phones, Facebook, Twitter and email. They consolidated into collective expressions rather than a tactical objective. Thus, in Egypt, the protesters who did flood onto the streets did not attempt to seize the Presidential palace. Instead, their communicative acts coalesced into that extraordinary physical statement of the crowds in Tahrir Square. When protesters faced up to the organized violent pro-Mubarak incursion into the demonstration, it was resisted in a collective but relatively spontaneous way.

The diffuse, horizontal nature of these movements made them very difficult to break. Their diversity and flexibility gave them an organic strength. They were networks, not organizations. Media, especially networked communications, were critical to making this happen. This is new. Levels of Internet penetration and mobile telephony in the Middle East have increased rapidly in the last few years.[13] This has given people new tools for political expression and activism. What is significant is that these new tools are different because they are networkable. This suits the kind of politics that appears to be emerging – not just in developing countries either. There seems to be a similar shift in developed countries towards less rigidly defined political movements. But it is particularly effective in relatively authoritarian regimes that are historically well prepared to crush opposition that manifests itself as a block (opposition party) or individual (dissenter). Sometimes these states find it harder to deal with diffuse networks of protest.

In their online state, these networks are made up of relatively 'weak' ties. These have been held up as less effective in achieving real-world political results:

> There is strength in weak ties, as the sociologist Mark Granovetter has observed. Our acquaintances – not our friends – are our greatest source of new ideas and information. The Internet lets us exploit the power of these kinds of distant connections with marvellous efficiency. It's terrific at the diffusion of innovation, interdisciplinary collaboration, seamlessly matching up buyers and sellers, and the logistical functions of the dating world. But weak ties seldom lead to high-risk activism.[14]

In the same article, Gladwell described how the actions of Civil Rights protesters back in 1960 in the Woolworth's lunch counter in Greensboro led to a 70,000-strong, region-wide physical protest: 'without e-mail, texting, Facebook, or Twitter'. Gladwell wrote that in October 2010, just as those networks were doing exactly what he declared they could not. The actions in spring 2011 were similar in their trajectory but, thanks in part to those derided social tools, much more rapid, pervasive and effective than the Civil Rights actions. They were more effective because they connected people in a way that was simultaneously personal and diffuse. This is much harder, but not impossible, for the authorities to control, because the key organizers become nodes, and nodes are harder to identify and control. Once neutralized, they are also much easier to replace. As we have seen, the networks that connect through weak ties can also be converted in a relatively short period into a public, real-world manifestation with impact.

When we look at how the activists and citizens used social networks in these situations, we can see how it was different from previous forms of political activist communication that were linear, vertical, directed. The flash mobs, data maps, texting, blogs and tweeting were not directed by a conventionally organized campaign. These were fluid, personalized, interactive, peer-authenticated communications that promoted personal engagement and collective endeavour.

Social media embody the connection between action and expression. For example, you can Tweet that you are going to a demonstration. The hashtag connects you to others and acts as an expression of your opinion, a call to action, and builds solidarity. It is democratic, efficient and endlessly variable. It is personal, but it increases social capital for the movement. Social media also work well with one of the most significant political communications practices, especially in urban areas – word of mouth – as well as when they become networked into mainstream media.

The most high-profile example captures many of these elements. Egyptian Facebook executive Wael Ghonim was in Dubai when he set up the Facebook page to commemorate a victim of Egyptian police brutality, 'We are all Khaled Said'. On his return to Egypt, Ghonim was himself imprisoned. His family publicized his case on regional satellite TV while bloggers rallied support. On his release, he in turn became an online video phenomenon after an emotional political outburst during a mainstream TV interview. He was unusual in that he became a personal focus for the uprising, but he resisted claiming any personal political leadership role. That preserved his value as a catalyst rather than an object of the networked activism.

We still need to know much more about the role of social media in challenging power in the 2011 Arab uprisings. Implicit in that assessment is also what results there are over the medium and long term. Networked protest may be effective in certain conditions in the short term, but does it create sustainable structures for consolidating change? However, in terms of the media's role in political disruption, it is enough to understand that they had an initial role in destabilizing existing power structures and expressing political energies for reform. As we begin to identify a new typology of media and networked political change, we can see how what happened contrasts with WikiLeaks. Both are networked enterprises, but while the social media movements were more diffuse, they were also much less vulnerable to capture or suppression. WikiLeaks lacked their transparency, connectivity and the participation of these open networks. In that sense the WikiLeaks network exploit is a mirror image of the closed systems that it seeks to disrupt, while the social media movements sought an alternative political ecology to the authoritarian regimes they challenged. What they have in common is an ability to exploit networks for political ends that challenge power.

## 4.3 WIKILEAKS – WHAT NEXT?

We have shown that WikiLeaks has changed in its short history, and as it moves forward it might change again. This is

not a stable project.* At the time of writing, Julian Assange
was planning to publish his ghost-written autobiography in
the autumn but was also waiting to hear the verdict of the
British courts on his removal to Sweden to face sexual assault
charges. Despite this personal drama, he insists that the
organization continues to function. There are regular fresh
WikiLeaks disclosures around the world. Although it may
feel more distant from its previous mainstream media partners in London and New York, its collaborations with *Dawn*
newspapers in Pakistan[15] and the *Hindu* in India[16] have had
real political impact by delving into its vast unpublished cache
of US Embassy cables. But what of the immediate future of
WikiLeaks itself? The challenge from new media 'sceptics'
such as Paul Starr[17] and John Lloyd was for the digital innovators to come up with lasting formats or organizations that
would replace the declining analogue or hard-copy mainstream media institutions: 'Without that, it's hard to see how
it could keep going: or at least, the nature of news collection
and news dissemination would have to be rethought – and
(in my view) another organizational structure or structures
would have to be invented which reproduced at least some of
the elements [of mainstream media institutions].'[18]

While its future will always be in doubt, WikiLeaks
does seem to be at a relatively defined stage where we can
assess it by Lloyd's criteria. It has become a kind of new
Networked (or mutualized[19]) News agency. It is no longer
a simple whistle-blower website. It is more than a raw news
wholesaler because it filters the information it receives. Just
like a mainstream news agency such as Reuters, it controls
the flow of data and channels it to certain outlets, includ-

---

* See the Epilogue for a summary of the latest and highly significant
developments on these issues at the end of August 2011 when WikiLeaks
released all the Embassy cables in full.

ing its own website. However, while this is journalistic in its methods, it is, in practice, limited to selection and redaction. WikiLeaks does not re-version or package the material as it did, exceptionally, with the Collateral Murder video. Nor does it produce much analysis of, or commentary on, the material. It does not provide significant background, context or references. On its own website it does not allow inter-activity, let alone the highly searchable and participatory data visualizations that have been a feature of the publication by its collaborators such as the *Guardian* and *New York Times*. It claims to have received new material but it is not clear whether it has established a sustainable supply of fresh sources with significant stories. Some of those who have collaborated with WikiLeaks, but who have also been critical of its practices and values, play down its longer-term importance as well as its short-term prospects: 'Nor is it clear to me that WikiLeaks represents some kind of cosmic triumph of transparency. If the official allegations are to be believed, most of WikiLeaks's great revelations came from a single anguished Army private.'[20]

By mid-2011, the bulk of WikiLeaks' own production and packaging effort related in large part to campaigning material about the house arrest and extradition case of Julian Assange. This included a video detailing the placement of three cameras around the property to which Assange was bailed. It implied that Assange was being subjected to sophisticated surveillance. Embarrassingly, just days after WikiLeaks released its video, the devices were shown to be traffic speed monitors, containing no cameras, which had been in place for eight years.[21] WikiLeaks has a small staff and very little of the institutional infrastructure that Lloyd lists, such as training, marketing and legal support. Its 'collective memory, a clear goal, ideals'[22] appear to be embedded almost entirely in the person of Assange himself.

Some have suggested that WikiLeaks could develop institutional substance by becoming a more formal transparency NGO. It is a choice, says Evgeny Morozov, between a deliberately alternative, outsider role and a more integrated, mainstream function:

> WikiLeaks could continue moving in the more sensible direction that, in some ways, it is already on: collaborating with traditional media, redacting sensitive files, and offering those in a position to know about potential victims of releases the chance to vet the data. It is a choice between WikiLeaks becoming a new Red Brigades, or a new Transparency International.[23]

If it became a 'Transparency International' NGO, WikiLeaks would gain legitimacy and institutional influence. It would bring it into the same media space of advocacy journalism that other human rights NGOs are increasingly occupying, including one called, indeed, Transparency International. As we have seen above in the section on 'WikiLeaks as a model' (section 3.3), this is not an entirely problem-free space. However, Morozov seems to be suggesting that there is a role for a more political agency that would use the release of unclassified information in more responsible and strategic ways. That would mean building capacity with increased income and management structures and even some sort of constitutional arrangement that might include accountability and governance mechanisms. It would also mean increasing its journalistic and campaigning staff resource: 'One could only hope that the lesson he would draw from all this is not that WikiLeaks had not released enough documents but that, in order to be truly effective, any releases of documents needed to be accompanied by dedicated investigative reporting and strategic and careful advocacy.'[24]

As was put to Morozov in a live debate, this would 'take all the fun out' of the project.[25] More seriously, perhaps it is the lack of structure that gives WikiLeaks its capacity to take risks, resist censorship, and avoid capture by particular interests or being influenced by institutional relationships. It is also what Assange wants. He seems incapable or unwilling to build WikiLeaks as an institution that has capacity beyond his immediate control. On the other hand, he does not advocate a 'Red Brigades' model either. His is a vision of disruption that does not rule out violent consequences, but advocates disruption rather than terror as a methodology. He places WikiLeaks as an alternative power within a network of information in which corporate and governmental interests are increasingly becoming aligned. This is why he describes Facebook as the 'most appalling spy machine that has ever been invented':

> Here we have the world's most comprehensive database about people, their relationships, their names, their addresses, their locations, their communications with each other, and their relatives, all sitting within the United States, all accessible to US Intelligence ... it's not a matter of serving a subpoena, they have an interface they have developed for US Intelligence to use. Now, is the case that Facebook is run by US Intelligence? No, it's not like that. It's simply that US Intelligence is able to bring to bear legal and political pressure on them ... It's costly for them to hand out individual records, one by one, so they have automated the process.[26]

So WikiLeaks is not a total transparency platform. As Assange has always insisted, transparency is not a goal, it is a method of achieving 'justice': 'It is not our goal to achieve a more transparent society; it's our goal to achieve a more just society. And most of the times, transparency and openness tends to lead in that direction, because abusive plans or behavior get opposed.'[27]

WikiLeaks is a network exploit that seeks to resist power through selective disclosure, and the degree or kind of revelation is relative to the power it assaults: 'Transparency should be proportional to the power that one has. The more power one has, the greater the dangers generated by that power, and the more need for transparency. Conversely, the weaker one is, the more danger there is in being transparent.'[28]

There is still significant public support for that kind of 'irresponsible' journalism that catches both the authorities and mainstream media off-guard. Governments have condemned WikiLeaks for the damage it does to the integrity of their information systems. They have warned that disclosures can jeopardize lives and imperil sensitive diplomatic operations. Mainstream journalists likewise have expressed fears that WikiLeaks could create a freedom-of-expression backlash. Yet, with rising levels of public scepticism about both mainstream media and governments, WikiLeaks chimes with a less deferential public mood. Mainstream media may adopt some of its techniques and will continue to be tempted by collaboration. However, they will struggle to replicate that function of the risk-taking challenge to power. So there is still a gap in the market for relatively reckless and fairly immune whistle-blowers. It is not clear, though, if WikiLeaks itself is going to be able to continue to produce the goods.

It is currently not a classic alternative media organization, nor is it a political or issue-based campaigning group. There is no evidence yet of any formal arrangement with other advocacy groups or NGOs, although this was supposed to have been part of the original make-up of WikiLeaks, and Assange has claimed more recently that NGOs will be part of a coalition that sustains it in the future. It is a hybrid entity that exploits the global digital information network both to source its material and to distribute it. While theoretically subject to legal and extra-legal actions, it has avoided sanctions and remains at one distinct remove from being a conventional media or political enterprise. Even the most diffuse global multi-national corporations and organizations have some kind of geographical base. Assange and WikiLeaks remain of no fixed abode. WikiLeaks looks set to continue with its model of an independent organization that enters into collaboration with other media to process and publish classified information – transnational, if not transitory.

## 4.4 CONCLUSION: WIKILEAKS, NETWORKED JOURNALISM AND POWER

WikiLeaks is very much what people think it is. As we have seen, it has changed. It is not transparent. So it is difficult to understand empirically. It has also been subject to radically different interpretations, depending on varying political, cultural or professional perspectives. Former Vice Presidential candidate Sarah Palin saw it as a terrorist organization.[29] Conversely, a Norwegian MP has nominated it for a Nobel Peace Prize.[30] It has also been subject to varying narrative constructions. Julian Assange and his associates deliberately conjured up the illusion in the early days that WikiLeaks had a vast staff. Assange continues to evoke the myth of an idealistic radical enterprise with himself as the victimized but noble figurehead. Mass media gleefully accepted this invitation to personalize its coverage of the quirky white-haired Australian and his mysterious website. When the leaks became more high-profile, mainstream media continued to frame the story through the figure of Assange, culminating in the relentlessly detailed focus on the sexual assault allegations. Underpinning this was the mass media framing of WikiLeaks – especially, but not exclusively, in America – as a threat to the integrity of the state and an enemy combatant in the so-called 'War On Terror'. It is possible that this was partly because mainstream media took a while to understand the new context and the potential alignment of interest between themselves and WikiLeaks. According to media and technology analyst John Naughton, this was not in their own interest:

> Mainstream media mostly got this wrong in all kinds of ways – they connived in the framing of the story about WikiLeaks as part of the global terror threat to the United States. They pretended there was something different about what WikiLeaks did and what 'proper' journalism should do and they concentrated to an obsessive degree on Julian Assange personally and ignored the treatment of Bradley Manning, and they perpetuated the falsehood that 250,000 cables had been dumped thoughtlessly. And they dug their own graves by continuing to insist that WikiLeaks was not proper journalism, because the legal and extra-legal attacks on WikiLeaks, if continued, will impact more widely on freedom of expression.[31]

Even when the cables revealed matters of substance, it was difficult to move the mainstream media coverage from the drama of the process to the actual issues. This was partly about professional rivalry. Newspapers are reluctant to follow up on a rival's scoop. Also, the issues were complex and the volume of information vast. So they did not fit easily into the more reactive agenda and short format of most mainstream news bulletins and front pages. In America and Britain the Iraq revelations were seen as largely historic, while even the Embassy cables were part of a global agenda rather than domestic politics. This may have been less the case in countries like India where the revelations did have real impact on parliamentary proceedings because they became part of internal political disputes and discourses. So the WikiLeaks of 2010 were a challenge to the ability of even its willing mainstream partners to tell such big stories. It exposed the limits of conventional news.

WikiLeaks has acted as a site for various intersections between media and power, and as an actor itself. WikiLeaks has made us reconsider how politics and journalism work. It also makes us think again about its future. But ultimately its real value may be to show that the very nature of journalism and news has changed from a socio-economic structure that produces journalism as an object, to a contestable, unstable networked process, especially in its relation to power.

WikiLeaks is an innovative enterprise, but it is a hybrid that draws upon quite traditional ideas as well as practices enabled by new technologies. Compared to many media organizations, it has a relatively limited functionality, albeit combined with a global reach and, when in collaboration, a huge audience. It is made possible by the shift in the nature of our information society. It is enabled by new technologies in a practical and systematic way. Whether it survives or not, it heralds a profound shift according to network theorists:

> In a certain sense, these 'colossal' WikiLeaks disclosures can simply be explained as a consequence of the dramatic spread of IT usage, together with a dramatic drop in its costs, including those for the storage of millions of documents. Another contributing factor is the fact that safekeeping state and corporate secrets – never mind private ones – has become rather difficult in an age of instant reproducibility and dissemination. WikiLeaks here becomes symbolic for

a transformation in the 'information society' at large, and holds up a mirror of future things to come.[32]

We are familiar now with how those technological developments have radically altered the practice of journalism in the Internet era: lower barriers of entry, personalization, interactivity, globalization, 24/7 consumption, multi-skilled producers working on a multi-layered non-linear process. The list of changing conditions goes on. Structurally, the creation of news is being transformed from the manufacture of information products to the provision of information services. We are moving from a period of contained, linear transfers of data and analysis to more accessible network flows. In response, journalists have to acquire new skills, such as numeracy, and fresh attitudes, such as a willingness to encourage public participation. News organizations are changing their structures into more collaborative, networked forms of production and publication. The revenue mechanism may be a subscription or a pay-wall, advertising or a grant from a foundation, but the news-gathering and dissemination are networked and, no matter how discrete and closed the editorial operation might be, it operates in a wider universe of networked information. Sources and audiences are becoming networked directly into those information flows, and thus are disintermediating conventional news organizations' traditional role as the main discoverer or assigner of sources and the distributor of their meaning.

WikiLeaks demonstrates the key aspect of that shift in the production and nature of news. It exists as a network exploit. It takes advantage of the affordances of the network. So, in this case, it is able both to be connected to the wider mainstream media and yet to preserve its discrete identity: 'WikiLeaks did not just move information from one place to another on the information network. They exploited another system, the [mainstream] media system within the network. That is what makes it important. It was not until they fed that information into the existing media system that the leaks became significant, that is what makes it an exploit of network power.'[33]

The fact that this process created tension and friction between WikiLeaks and its mainstream media partners merely emphasizes the novelty and challenge that the network exploit produced for all participants.[34]

So, according to a media ethnographer, WikiLeaks is symptomatic of how the relationship between the news organization and the source has changed:

> The idea that a source – and in this case I'm referring to Julian Assange as a source, because that's how news organizations see him – is working with multiple news outlets simultaneously; the fact that he is able to withdraw cooperation with particular news outlets if they do something that he doesn't like, is very new; [and] that affects how journalism gets produced.[35]

The Internet and networked news communications are changing the idea of 'news' itself. This may be more profound than simply a rearrangement of the structure of the industry or production. News as the reporting of 'breaking stories' or new events is no longer controlled or defined by mainstream journalism. Now it is happening all around us in networks in which citizens and journalists act as curators, connectors and facilitators, as well as in the traditional roles of reporters, analysts and investigators. It can be accidental, as when CCTV records a plane hitting the Pentagon. Or it can be automatic, as with the reporting of much financial market data. Potentially, anything that happens, anything expressed, can instantly be made visible as a communication act by anyone and transmitted anywhere. That loss of the ownership of news for mainstream media has also challenged traditional ideas for framing journalistic discourse.

WikiLeaks is an example of the new forms of journalism that are emerging from and reshaping the news ecology and the nature of news itself. For example, classic ideas of objectivity or impartiality constructed in the age of mass mainstream media in the nineteenth and twentieth centuries are being replaced by notions of accountability and interactivity. WikiLeaks is changing, in particular, the conception and practice of investigative or scandal-centred journalism. Instead of a partial, one-off revelation that allows a brief insight into the structure of power, we are given a sustained and extensive view of how it works as well as what it thinks and does. Instead of a selective quote or a document that the journalist inserts into a revelatory narrative, we are given the whole source direct. The cables, for example, even with partial release, were a wide-ranging exposure of the American diplomatic system in comparison to, for example, the selective tip-offs that drove part of the Watergate investigation.

This may be a question of degree. Are we simply getting much more? It certainly changes the expectations of readers. They now assume that power can and should be transparent and that the transparency should be relatively unmediated. A shaky video from an eyewitness on YouTube can have as much authenticity and authority as a beautifully directed documentary film. The public also appears to expect more from journalism beyond that transparency. In a world where the citizen can, theoretically at least, access news directly, journalism as a practice must offer more added value – such as packaging, filtering, explanation or relevance. That value can also be added through the news organization's own resources or through the network. Thus this networked information environment offers the potential for much more

contextualized news that is more connected into other expertise. The professional journalist may have specialist skills, but
they do not need to know everything. Instead, they have to
be connected to people who will value the information and
potentially add value to it. An academic paper by a group of
American political geographers showed how the WikiLeaks
Afghanistan war logs had improved their interpretation of
that conflict:

> Efforts to make sense of ongoing wars by most commenta-
> tors (apart from individuals who have served in government
> agencies) chiefly rely on media accounts of the conflict;
> they spend immense amounts of time and resources trying
> to penetrate the texts of unclassified and declassified gov-
> ernment documents, and official and non-governmental
> agency reports. As a result of the uncertain reliability of
> these sources, policy suggestions and academic analysis are
> always subject to the criticism that the data from which con-
> clusions are drawn have been falsified or are biased, uneven
> in coverage, amnesiac about certain subjects, or exculpatory
> of government decisions. The unexpurgated [WikiLeaks]
> war logs offer a ground-level view of the fighting, with each
> row in the enormous database corresponding to an event
> for which a report is filed.[36]

Journalists should see this kind of response as a resource, not
an end result.

This kind of journalism does not mean that all news
becomes complex and deep. It may even be the opposite. As
we see a trend towards faster and more reactive mainstream
news, this kind of more networked, transparency-data-
revelation journalism will be increasingly valued, but still
an alternative. However, it may not thrive when it exists set
apart from mainstream media. Even when the public has

open access to networks of information, it does not always pay attention. WikiLeaks' initial pure leaking strategy simply did not have the effect that Assange and his colleagues expected:

> They were baffled by what happened. They put all this information up and then what they expected to happen did not. Governments did not fall, banks did not collapse. Nobody actually seemed to be taking much notice. It's very difficult to trust information when it's decoupled from its context. It was indigestible raw information that was very discouraging to look at and nobody knew where it had come from, so creating a paradox that defeated their own objects.[37]

WikiLeaks only got through to the modern, connected public when it shifted from simply publishing information to publishing information plus context plus explanation and on a platform with a predisposed audience. WikiLeaks hoped to profit from the disintermediation of news by connecting directly with the public. By doing so, it also changed its publication style to one that incorporated information with context and explanation. That shift seemed to suggest that the global audience still enjoys the efficiencies of more traditional editorial production.

This situation contains an irony: it was only by acting like a pre-network-era mainstream news organization that WikiLeaks became able to leverage its network. Just as the newspaper was once the conduit – or the pinch point – between, say, politicians and the public, WikiLeaks made itself the chokepoint between the conventional media and the information they wanted to access. Perhaps just by being in the right place at the right time, WikiLeaks highlighted the strength both of disrupting the Internet's information networks and of leveraging the position long enjoyed by mainstream news organizations.

Where there is an action like WikiLeaks, there will be a reaction. The state and other forms of authority have attempted to reassert control, and online networks are not immune from that. Indeed, part of the process might be an alliance between corporate and governmental interests in order to close the web:

> WikiLeaks has taken advantage of a gap in state surveillance technology . . . and the state will inevitably fight back when you start finding its secrets . . . we can expect an attempt at a greater level of censorship . . . changes in legislation at an international level and we can expect a stepping up of research into surveillance techniques online . . . privacy of individuals will be used as a stalking horse for these changes.[38]

Some would welcome a retrenchment as a necessary part of re-balancing the needs of power for a degree of confidentiality for its efficient and responsible operation with the right to freedom of expression: 'Like equality and freedom, we must balance the conflicting goods of secretiveness and transparency. . . . I am fairly sure that WikiLeaks won't be with us for the long haul, and that those who imitate its innovations will be more constrained and responsible.'[39]

However, this idea of WikiLeaks as an aberration fails to recognize the wider changes in the terms of trade of power and information. Any network contains the seeds of resistance in it,[40] but is WikiLeaks a prototype for journalism that will hold networked power to account in a thorough, sustainable and democratic way? What can WikiLeaks and the new networked disruptive journalism do for local journalism, for example? Will the attention given to revealing swathes of classified detail in beautiful data visualizations distract from the expensive and laborious task of long-term investigative journalism? WikiLeaks is by no means the cause of the threat to mainstream quality journalism, but it may be symptomatic of a failure to attend to the need for journalism as a quotidian as well as exceptional activity. If journalism is to fulfil its role in fostering a healthy civic society, then it has a more general duty to report on the more mundane and pervasive actions of power. So, for example, independent hyper-local news sites can be more effective than traditional local journalism at critiquing power at a grass-roots level, but their actual capacity to do so is still nowhere near that offered by commercial or public-sector journalism.

The real business of journalism cannot just be this kind of mega-leak. It is the forensic long-term investigation of petty malpractice and unglamorous injustice, such as the abuse of the elderly in care homes. The search for the spectacular may not impede this journalism but it certainly distracts attention from it. We still need journalists to dig up stories, not just wait for them to be released. Watergate was not just a leak, it was patient pushing and door-knocking too.

Society also needs 'outsider' journalism to challenge media and power. In liberal, open societies, a sustainable, reflexive democratic political culture is, paradoxically, fostered by the challenge of those who see themselves as excluded and who wish to attack and undermine the status quo. This is the role of what Muhlmann calls a 'Journalism that is aware of the importance of its political role in democracy, that is, is sensitive to a twofold requirement: to form a community and create an "us", and to sustain the conflict without which democracy dies.'[41] As we have seen, Julian Assange asserts that WikiLeaks is part of the tradition of radical journalism that seeks not just to reveal uncomfortable or disturbing facts, but also to change society and shift power. He is what Muhlmann would call a 'decentring' journalist, like George Orwell, who does not seek merely to record the deficiencies of society, but to mobilize change. Yet, as Muhlmann shows, the history of challenging journalism inevitably ends in accommodation through the process of communication:

> The decentring journalist wants to make us, the public, see something that is 'other' to us, question us, and change us; this requires that, by one means or another, a connection is established between it and us. But is this connection not inconsistent with the fact that it is something 'other' that is at issue? Are we not, in the end, decentred by an otherness that is always partly tamed?[42]

For some, WikiLeaks is best not tamed. For 'cyber-optimists' such as Clay Shirky, WikiLeaks is 'our Amsterdam', a rallying point in the battle for an open Internet and freedom of expression in general. Whatever its particular failings, it represents, in its irresponsibility, a space for reform and progress: 'The practical history of politics . . . suggests that the periodic appearance of such unconstrained actors in the short haul is essential to increased democratization, not just of politics but of thought.'[43]

As Shirky points out, those sixteenth-century Dutch printers who helped to unleash the forces of scientific inquiry and democratic politics upon the Catholic Church ended up subject to 'restrictions on libel, the publication of trade secrets, and sedition' that were all based on law. So the modern Western information society emerged. The political question at the end of this book is whether WikiLeaks and the threat of the new news presage a comparable historic moment. There is always a danger of confusing novelty with revolution, especially in media:

With the Internet, we tend to like to believe that everything is new all the time. The difference with WikiLeaks, as
opposed to earlier battles between the open web and government, is a difference in degree. The amount of data is
greater, the collaboration with news organizations is new,
the impact of that data is greater, so the real question is
when does a difference in degree equal a difference in kind.
And have we reached the moment where difference in
degree has now tipped over into a difference in kind?[44]

Ultimately, there is no scientific measure that allows us
to confirm or deny the hypothesis of a profound change in
media – let alone politics – brought about by WikiLeaks
and the other new networked political communications. We
are still in a transitional period, what Lovink describes as: 'a
"pilot" phase in an evolution towards a far more generalized
culture of anarchic exposure, beyond the traditional politics
of openness and transparency'.[45]

Most digital pilots fail. WikiLeaks might, too. This serves
to remind us that the idea of the radical voice and the critical
witness changes as media history moves on, just as mainstream media change. The new news is new because the
network is a new context. It has created, for now, an age
of uncertainty both for power and for opposition to power.
Deliberate disruption by hackers, leakers and politically radical news activists is part of that uncertainty. The evolution
of network dissent is both part of keeping the network open
and a function of its openness.

Journalism has always changed in its organization and its
nature. This is partly a reflection of social change and historical circumstance as well as of technological innovation.
Every time this happens there are innovators and disruptors
who, in Schumpeter's phrase, destroy creatively and sometimes create disruptively.[46] Julian Assange and WikiLeaks

have been carried by contemporary currents of communication change, but they have also contributed an enterprise
that is both significant and effective. In our view, WikiLeaks
may well not survive, and in retrospect its revelations will
be seen as large but hardly decisive. WikiLeaks itself will
be seen as significant and symptomatic but not, in itself,
game-changing.

The partisan approach to judging WikiLeaks has plagued
the debate and prevented mainstream journalists and politicians from learning from the experience. Speaking as
journalists, we would argue that, instead of taking sides,
we should be taking notice. Julian Assange is not the first
journalist to have eccentric habits and a huge ego. He may
or may not deserve moral or legal censure. But in the end,
the WikiLeaks episode and its significance is not about
Julian Assange but about democracy and the citizen and the
role of journalism in our networked age. The threat is not
WikiLeaks and the new networked news, it is still secrecy
and the abuse of power.

# EPILOGUE

At the end of August 2011, as this book was going to print, WikiLeaks finally began the publication of all of the Embassy cables online in unredacted form.[1] This meant that all the cables released through partnerships with mainstream media would now be available unedited. All the unreleased cables would be accessible in full. The effort made by WikiLeaks staff, and journalists working for their mainstream media partners, to protect individuals, such as informants, by editing out potentially dangerous details was rendered pointless. For example, Associated Press identified ninety confidential American sources, including human rights workers based in authoritarian regimes who were now identifiable.[2] More than 1,000 cables contained references marked 'STRICTLY PROTECT', a designation used by the Americans to mark at-risk sources. As we showed in chapters 2 and 3, Julian Assange had appeared to accept, however reluctantly, that as publishers of the information WikiLeaks did have a degree of responsibility for the effects of disclosure. The August

2011 unredacted release appears to contradict that, in practice and possibly also in principle.

This huge data disclosure also meant that WikiLeaks' most recent 'business' strategy of gradual release was abandoned. The vast cache of 251,287 documents was now to become available to anyone online. It meant that WikiLeaks had, in a sense, reverted to its early model as a pure whistle-blower website, a publisher of last resort, that put data online in its full, raw state. It appeared to be a reaffirmation of its founding principles of total disclosure regardless of the resistance of the authorities and the objections of mainstream media. It could also, however, be seen as an admission of failure.

On its website, it said the dramatic action was 'Due to recent attacks on our infrastructure'. WikiLeaks said it was forced to take this step because other people had now disclosed the password and the file location and it was only a matter of time before the data were disclosed fully anyway. WikiLeaks said that it was an accelerated publication that was designed 'to get as much of the material as possible into the hands of journalists and human rights lawyers who need it'.[3] WikiLeaks had polled its followers on Twitter to ask whether they should go ahead with the release. Unsurprisingly, WikiLeaks' social media followers were enthusiasts for total publication. However, this whole process was something of an acknowledgement of reality as the cables had in fact already been made available by a bizarre series of mistakes made by WikiLeaks and its former staff and media partners.

The exact circumstances are in dispute[4] (a dispute that includes the role of *Guardian* journalist and former WikiLeaks staffer James Ball, who has co-written this book). But it appears that a combination of incompetence and clever 'hacktavist' investigation led to the security of the files containing the documents being breached. As we showed in section 2.4, WikiLeaks lost complete control of the files during the process of partnership with the mainstream media, through an internal action. The password for the file was also used as a chapter heading by *Guardian* journalist David Leigh in his book about the newspaper's collaboration with WikiLeaks.[5] Leigh claims he was told that the password was only temporary. WikiLeaks made no complaint about the chapter heading until 24 hours before it published the unredacted cables. Despite claiming to have been aware of the security concern for 2 months, Assange made no mention of any concerns during a 90-minute face-to-face meeting with *Guardian* editor Alan Rusbridger on 4 August.

A member of WikiLeaks' staff had, in December 2010, placed encrypted copies of numerous files in the WikiLeaks archive online as a form of back-up, apparently re-using a series of files with well-known 'master passwords' known by several ex-supporters. The full Embassy cables file was included. When this became known, people were able to work out the password through complicated investigative work – aided, according to WikiLeaks, by the publication of the password in the *Guardian*'s book. German magazine *Freitag*[6] published an article informed by one activist who was keen to point out this lapse in WikiLeak's security. It pointed to the existence of the file and its vulnerable state, but did not disclose any information leading towards the password or the file's location. WikiLeaks then published a series of tweets denying failings on its own part. The detail in those tweets may have helped a small group of Internet activists to find the files, which were subsequently, and perhaps as a result, published in a difficult-to-access format on the rival leak site Cryptome. In the end it was Julian Assange's decision to publish the files in an easily accessible format on the WikiLeaks site.

The recriminations were bitter. WikiLeaks and its supporters attacked the *Guardian* and former WikiLeaks staffer Daniel Domscheit-Berg in particular.[7] On the other hand, mainstream media critics saw the unredacted disclosure as proof that WikiLeaks was essentially irresponsible. Most mainstream news outlets chose to report the security breach rather than the contents of the cables. WikiLeaks' former mainstream media business partners signed a common statement condemning the release.[8] Although WikiLeaks had that meeting with *Guardian* editor Alan Rusbridger in early August, it was clear that after this episode the relationship with the *Guardian* was at rock-bottom. But so now was WikiLeaks' reputation for competence and responsibility. It found itself once more firmly outside the pale of mainstream media codes. It might be that it felt more comfortable there. Ethically, its supporters have argued that far more people have died in wars started by US diplomats covered uncritically by mainstream media than will be harmed by the unredacted release of the cables. However, editorial ethics is not a game of equivalence. At this point, it does seem that WikiLeaks had either changed its moral stance (again) or was technically incapable of acting in accordance with its principles.

This episode impacts on WikiLeaks' evolution. It does not rule out future acts of networked journalism with WikiLeaks acting as a source for mainstream media outlets, but it certainly makes them less likely. Several WikiLeaks supporters have suggested the *Guardian* and other mainstream outlets have acted naïvely or petulantly during collaboration with the site, but ultimately responsibility for this release does not lie with them. The challenge for mainstream media organizations looking to work with WikiLeaks in the future is to find any way to attach credibility to assurances by WikiLeaks that they will not eventually publish full, unredacted, archives of material. Other mainstream editors may be tempted by the offer of secrets in the future but WikiLeaks' dream of an endless supply of willing mass media platforms may be over.

It also does not rule out WikiLeaks pursuing a version of the transparency NGO model – although it is interesting that press freedom group Reporters Without Borders, which had been a WikiLeaks supporter, ended its technical support and condemned the release.[9] WikiLeaks appears further away than ever from being ready to assume the organizational responsibilities of becoming a properly constituted, accountable public body. So it seems most likely to continue with its unusual, if not unique, hybrid role, tied closely to the fate of its editor, Julian Assange.

There is quite probably interesting and important material in the newly released cables, and as people sift through them they might well contribute to a fuller understanding of how global power works. We will probably never know whether the unredacted nature of the release leads to the suffering of innocent individuals or to more systematic damage to blameless organizations or movements. Some former WikiLeaks enthusiasts are now writing it off.[10] This feels too hasty. There is real value in having whistle-blowing sites. Neither the new communications technology nor the complex geopolitical circumstances that made WikiLeaks possible are going away. Mainstream media and conventional politics should and will continue to be challenged. As we suggested in chapter 4, WikiLeaks is not and will not be the only form of disruptive journalism in the networked news era. But is this the best or even a sustainable version? In practice, much may depend upon the judicial process around Julian Assange himself. However, the real damage to WikiLeaks following this latest action may come from its credibility with those who might have provided it with future material. Will anyone trust them with a serious leak again?

# NOTES

## Introduction

1 J. Rosen, 2010, 'The Afghanistan War Logs Released By WikiLeaks, the World's First Stateless News Organization', PressThink Blog, viewed 21 June 2011, http://pressthink.org/2010/07/the-afghanistan-war-logs-released-by-WikiLeaks-the-worlds-first-stateless-news-organization/. (Except in the Epilogue, all websites cited in the notes were last accessed on 1 June 2011, unless otherwise stated.)

## 1 What was new about WikiLeaks?

1 S. Richmond, 2010, 'Jimmy Wales: People Think I'm Responsible for WikiLeaks', *Telegraph*, 11 August, http://blogs.telegraph.co.uk/technology/shanerichmond/100005434/jimmy-wales-people-think-im-responsible-for-WikiLeaks/.

2 C. Shirky, 2009, *Here Comes Everybody: How Change Happens When People Come Together*, London: Penguin Books.

3 WikiLeaks, 2008, 'WikiLeaks: About', http://web.archive.org/web/20081217112603/http://WikiLeaks.org/wiki/WikiLeaks:About#What_is_WikiLeaks.3F_How_does_WikiLeaks_oper te.3F.

4 Julian Assange quoted in *Cryptome*, 2006, 'WikiLeaks Leak',

*Cryptome*,    http://cryptome.org/WikiLeaks/WikiLeaks-leak. htm.

5 Anonymous is a specific group but it is a diffuse and porous network and also acts as a synecdote for a wider movement. See http://en.wikipedia.org/wiki/Anonymous_(group).

6 S. Dreyfus, 1997, *Underground: Tales of Hacking, Madness, and Obsession on the Electronic Frontier*, Kew: Mandarin Australia.

7 S. Dreyfus, 2001, 'Underground: Tales of Hacking, Madness, and Obsession on the Electronic Frontier', The Project Gutenberg,    www.gutenberg.org/cache/epub/4686/pg4686. html.

8 Ibid.

9 D. Domscheit-Berg, 2011, *Inside WikiLeaks: My Time With Julian Assange at the World's Most Dangerous Website*, New York: Crown Publishers, p. 80.

10 N. Barrowclough, 2010, 'The Secret Life of WikiLeaks Founder Julian Assange', *Sydney Morning Herald*, 22 May, www.smh.com.au/technology/technology-news/the-secret-life-of-WikiLeaks-founder-julian-assange-20100521-w1um. html.

11 Chaos Computer Club, www.ccc.de/en/.

12 Cryptome, 'WikiLeaks Leak'.

13 Ibid.

14 Ibid.

15 John Young, ibid.

16 Wikipedia, 2011, 'Brute-force Attack', 10 June, viewed 27 June 2011, http://en.wikipedia.org/wiki/Brute-force_attack.

17 WikiLeaks, 2007, 'The Looting of Kenya under President Moi', August, http://WikiLeaks.org/wiki/Media/The_looting_of_Kenya.

18 C. Cadwalladr, 2010, 'Julian Assange, Monk of the Online Age Who Thrives on Intellectual Battle', *Guardian*, 1 August, www. guardian.co.uk/media/2010/aug/01/julian-assange-WikiLeaks-afghanistan.

19 J. Rosen, 2010, 'The Afghanistan War Logs Released by WikiLeaks, the World's First Stateless News Organisation', PressThink Blog, 26 July, viewed 21 June 2011, http:// pressthink.org/2010/07/the-afghanistan-war-logs-released-by-WikiLeaks-the-worlds-first-stateless-news-organization/.

20  WikiLeaks, 'The Looting of Kenya under President Moi'.
21  C. Beckett, 2008, *SuperMedia: Saving Journalism So It Can Save the World*, Oxford: Wiley-Blackwell; C. Beckett, 2010, *The Value of Networked Journalism*, Polis Report, London: London School of Economics.
22  O. Bailey, C. Cammaerts and N. Carpentier, 2007, *Understanding Alternative Media*, Bucks.: Open University Press.
23  Amnesty International, 2009, 'Amnesty Announces Media Awards 2009 Winners', 2 June, http://amnesty.org.uk/news_details.asp?NewsID=18227.
24  Cryptome, http://cryptome.org/.
25  J. Assange, 2010, 'WikiLeaks Founder Julian Assange on the "War Logs"', *SPIEGEL*, 26 July, www.spiegel.de/international/world/0,1518,708518,00.html.
26  Domscheit-Berg, *Inside WikiLeaks*, pp. 45–59.
27  Assange quoted on http://svtplay.se/v/1984982.
28  J. Assange, 2010, Speech at the 2010 Oslo Freedom Forum, April, transcript available www.religiousforums.com/forum/political-debates/101236-transcript-julian-assange-WikiLeaks-speech-2010-a.html.
29  Brewster, 'Julien Assange from WikiLeaks – September 2009', Vimeo, http://vimeo.com/6710142.
30  O. Bailey, C. Cammaerts and N. Carpentier, 2007, *Understanding Alternative Media*, Bucks.: Open University Press, p. 29.
31  Beckett, *Supermedia*, pp. 9–40.
32  R. Greenslade, 2011, 'Loss-making Guardian Risks All on "Digital-first"', *London Evening Standard*, 22 June, viewed 22 June 2011, www.thisislondon.co.uk/markets/article-23963174-loss-making-guardian-risks-all-on-digital-first.do.
33  N. Davies, 2009, *Flat Earth News: An Award-Winning Reporter Exposes Falsehood, Distortion and Propaganda in the Global Media*, London: Random House UK.
34  J. Jarvis, 2007, 'New Rule: Cover What You Do Best. Link to the Rest', *Buzz Machine*, 22 February, www.buzzmachine.com/2007/02/22/new-rule-cover-what-you-do-best-link-to-the-rest/.
35  E. Schonfeld, 2009, 'Does Google Really Control the News?'

*TechCrunch*, 11 April, http://techcrunch.com/2009/04/11/does-google-really-control the-news/; K. Olmstead, A. Mitchell and T. Rosenstiel, 2011, 'Navigating News Online', *Journalism.org*, 9 May, www.journalism.org/analysis_report/navigating_news_online.

36 Beckett, *The Value of Networked Journalism*; B. Grueskin, A. Seave and L. Graves, 2011, *The Story So Far: What We Know About the Business of Digital Journalism*, New York: Columbia Journalism School.

37 J. Assange [attributed], 2006, 'Conspiracy as Governance', 3 December, http://cryptome.org/0002/ja-conspiracies.pdf.

38 Ibid.

39 R. Galloway and E. Thacker, 2007, *The Exploit* (Minnesota: University of Minnesota Press), pp. 81–97.

40 WikiLeaks, 2010, 'Collateral Murder', 5 April, www.collateral-murder.com.

41 T. Harnden, 2010, 'Julian Assange's Arrest Warrant: A Diversion from the Truth?' *Telegraph*, 22 August, www.telegraph.co.uk/technology/news/7959227/Julian-Assanges-arrest-warrant-a-diversion-from-the-truth.html.

42 Assange quoted in R. Khatchadourian, 2010, 'No Secrets', *New Yorker*, 7 June, www.newyorker.com/reporting/2010/06/07/100607fa_fact_khatchadourian?printable=true.

43 PolitiFact, 2010, 'Gates Said Leaked Military Video of Shooting in Iraq Doesn't Show the Broader Picture of Americans Being Fired Upon', *St Petersburg Times*, 12 April, www.politifact.com/truth-o-meter/statements/2010/apr/12/robert-gates/gates-said-leaked-military-video-shooting-iraq-doe/.

44 Rachelabombdotcom, 2010, 'Collateral Murder: White House Response', YouTube, 6 April, www.youtube.com/watch?v=UGQmhzRTIkM.

45 Khatchadourian, 'No Secrets'.

46 Cryptome, 2011, 'Birgitta Jonsdottir Interview on WikiLeaks', *Cryptome*, 2 March, http://cryptome.org/0003/jonsdottir-wl.htm.

## 2 The greatest story ever told? The Afghan war logs, Iraq war logs and the Embassy cables

1  M. Khalili. and E. Smith, 2010, 'Julian Assange on the Afghanistan War Logs: "They Show the True Nature of This War"', *Guardian*, 25 July, www.guardian.co.uk/world/video/2010/jul/25/julian-assange-WikiLeaks-interview-warlogs.

2  'Times Topics: Pentagon Papers', *New York Times*, http://topics.nytimes.com/top/reference/timestopics/subjects/p/pentagon_papers/index.html.

3  B. Farmer, 2010, 'WikiLeaks "to Release Video of US Strike on Afghan Civilians"', *Telegraph*, 11 April, www.telegraph.co.uk/news/worldnews/asia/afghanistan/7579132/WikiLeaks-to-release-video-of-US-strike-on-Afghan-civilians.html.

4  K. Poulsen and K. Zetter, 2010, '"I Can't Believe What I'm Confessing to You": The WikiLeaks Chats', *Wired*, 10 June, www.wired.com/threatlevel/2010/06/WikiLeaks-chat/.

5  N. Davies, 2009, *Flat Earth News: An Award-Winning Reporter Exposes Falsehood, Distortion and Propaganda in the Global Media*, London: Random House UK; O. Bailey, C. Cammaerts and N. Carpentier, 2007, *Understanding Alternative Media*, Bucks.: Open University Press.

6  M. Hosenball, 2011, 'U.S. Officials Privately Say WikiLeaks Damage Limited', *Reuters*, 18 January, www.reuters.com/article/2011/01/18/us-WikiLeaks-damage-idUSTRE70H6TO20110118.

7  CNN Wire, 2010, 'Gates: Posting Classified War Documents Was Morally Wrong', *CNN*, 1 August, http://edition.cnn.com/2010/POLITICS/08/01/gates.WikiLeaks/?hpt=T2#fbid=Uplw7ezfGkE.

8  S. Grey, 2006, *Ghost Plane*, New York: St Martin's Press.

9  Private research.

10  Sarah Ellison, www.vanityfair.com/politics/features/2011/02/the-guardian-201102?currentPage=4.

11  www.nytimes.com/2011/01/07/world/07wiki.html.

12  Received by one of the authors via email – text available: http://order-order.com/2010/11/26/that-WikiLeaks-d-notice/.

13  http://pewresearch.org/pubs/1820/media-coverage-WikiLeaks-state-department-cables.

14  www.bbc.co.uk/news/world-us-canada-11858895.

15  http://lieberman.senate.gov/index.cfm/news-events/news/2010/
    12/amazon-severs-ties-with-WikiLeaks.
16  www.washingtonpost.com/wp-dyn/content/article/2010/12/03
    /AR2010120306804.html.
17  http://WikiLeaks.ch/Media-Currently-Publishing.html.
18  D. Leigh and L. Harding, 2011, *WikiLeaks: Inside Julian
    Assange's War on Secrecy*, London: Guardian Books, p. 111.
19  Ibid.
20  R. Godec, 2010, 'US Embassy Cables: Tunisia – A US Foreign
    Policy Conundrum', *Guardian*, 7 December, www.guardian.
    co.uk/world/us-embassy-cables-documents/217138.
21  These comments are based on off-the-record conversations
    with State Department officials.
22  D. Domscheit-Berg, 2011, *Inside WikiLeaks: My Time With
    Julian Assange at the World's Most Dangerous Website*, New
    York: Crown Publishers.
23  *Telegraph*, 2010, 'Afghan War Logs: WikiLeaks Founder
    Defends Whistleblower Website', 26 July, www.telegraph.
    co.uk/news/worldnews/asia/afghanistan/7909889/Afghan-war-
    logs-WikiLeaks-founder-defends-whistleblower-website.html.
24  J. Assange, 2011, 'Of the People and for the People', *New
    Statesman*, 4 April, pp. 21–2.
25  P. Knightley, 2004, *The First Casualty: The War Correspondent
    as Hero and Myth-Maker from the Crimea to Iraq*, Maryland:
    Johns Hopkins University Press.
26  E. Herman and N. Chomsky, 1988, *Manufacturing Consent:
    The Political Economy of the Mass Media*, New York: Pantheon.
27  J. Assange [attributed], 2006, 'Conspiracy as Governance',
    *Cryptome*, 3 December, http://cryptome.org/0002/ja-conspira-
    cies.pdf.
28  H. Brooke, 2009, 'Unsung Hero', *Guardian*, 15 May, www.
    guardian.co.uk/politics/2009/may/15/mps-expenses-heather-
    brooke-foi; T. Steinberg, 2009, 'Blimey. "It Looks Like the
    Internets Won"', *mySociety*, 21 January, www.mysociety.org/
    2009/01/21/blimey-it-looks-like-the-internets-won/.
29  John Lloyd quoted in C. Beckett, 2011, 'Journalism and Power:
    The Importance of the Institution', *Polis Blog*, 27 June, http://
    blogs.lse.ac.uk/polis/2011/06/27/journalism-and-power-the-
    importance-of-the-institution/.

30 *New York Times* Editors, 2004, 'The *Times* and Iraq', *New York Times*, 26 May, www.nytimes.com/2004/05/26/international/middleeast/26FTE_NOTE.html?pagewanted=print.

31 W. Lippman, 1922, *Public Opinion*, New York: Free Press; J. Dewey 1927, *The Public and its Problems*, New York: Holt.

32 For a good dissection of the cant, see: A. Monck, 2008, *Can You Trust the Media?* Cambridge: Icon Books.

33 Index on Censorship, 2011, 'WikiLeaks, Belarus, and Israel Shamir', *Index on Censorship*, 5 February, www.indexoncensorship.org/2011/02/WikiLeaks-belarus-and-israel-shamir/.

### 3 WikiLeaks and the future of journalism

1 D. Domscheit-Berg, 2011, *Inside Wikileaks: My Time With Julian Assange at the World's Most Dangerous Website*, New York: Crown Publishers.

2 D. Leigh and L. Harding, 2011, *WikiLeaks: Inside Julian Assange's War On Secrecy*, London: Guardian Books.

3 Ibid.

4 www.guardian.co.uk/media/2011/jan/31/WikiLeaks-holocaust-denier-handled-moscow-cables.

5 April 2011 – Kensington Town Hall, organized by The Frontline Club.

6 J. Pilger, 2010, 'Protect Assange, Don't Abuse Him', *New Statesman*, 15 December, www.newstatesman.com/global-issues/2010/12/women-rights-pilger-assange.

7 J. Pilger, 2011, 'The War on WikiLeaks: A John Pilger Investigation and Interview with Julian Assange', *John Pilger.com*, 13 January, www.johnpilger.com/articles/the-war-on-WikiLeaks-a-john-pilger-investigation-and-interview-with-julian-assange.

8 L. Brooks, 2010, 'No One Gains from This "Rape-Rape Defence" of Julian Assange', *Guardian*, 9 December, www.guardian.co.uk/commentisfree/2010/dec/09/nobody-gains-from-misogynist-defence-of-assange.

9 Assange quoted in K. Poulsen and K. Zetter, 2010, 'Unpublished Iraq War Logs Trigger Internal WikiLeaks Revolt', *Wired*, 27 September, www.wired.com/threatlevel/2010/09/WikiLeaks-revolt/.

10  Geert Lovink quoted in A. Powell, 2011, 'The WikiLeaks Phenomenon and New Media Power', *The New Everyday*, 8 April, http://mediacommons.futureofthebook.org/tne/pieces/WikiLeaks-phenomenon-and-new-media-power.

11  Domscheit-Berg, *Inside WikiLeaks*, p. 3.

12  J. Pontin, 2011, 'Secrets and Transparency', *Technology Review*, 26 January, viewed 27 June 2011, www.technologyreview.com/blog/pontin/26314/?p1=A3.

13  N. Davies, 2010, '10 Days in Sweden: The Full Allegations against Julian Assange', *Guardian*, 17 December, www.guardian.co.uk/media/2010/dec/17/julian-assange-sweden.

14  D. Murphy, 2010, 'WikiLeaks' Julian Assange Issues Threat and Complains about . . . Leaks', *Christian Science Monitor*, 21 December, www.csmonitor.com/World/Global-Issues/2010/1221/WikiLeaks-Julian-Assange-issues-threat-and-complains-about-leaks.

15  'Julian Assange's Petard' [Editorial], 2010, *New York Sun*, 19 December, www.nysun.com/editorials/julian-assanges-petard/87174/.

16  D. Usborne, 2010, 'Assange is "High-tech Terrorist", Says Biden', *Independent*, 20 December, www.independent.co.uk/news/world/americas/assange-is-a-hitech-terrorist-says-biden-2164988.html.

17  E. Pilkington, 2011, *WikiLeaks: US Opens Grand Jury Hearing*, 11 May, www.guardian.co.uk/media/2011/may/11/us-opens-WikiLeaks-grand-jury-hearing.

18  K. Gosztola, 2011, 'Grand Jury Investigation into WikiLeaks Just Another Government "Fishing Expedition"', *Firedoglake*, 11 May, http://my.firedoglake.com/kgosztola/2011/05/11/grand-jury-investigation-into-WikiLeaks-just-another-government-fishing-expedition/.

19  C. Savage, 2010, 'Amazon Cites Terms of Use in Expulsion of WikiLeaks', *New York Times*, 2 December, www.nytimes.com/2010/12/03/world/03amazon.html.

20  F. Abrams, 2010, 'Why WikiLeaks is Unlike the Pentagon Papers', *Wall Street Journal*, 29 December, http://online.wsj.com/article/SB10001424052970204527804576044020396601528.html?.

21  B. Keller, 2011, 'Dealing with Assange and the WikiLeaks

Secrets', *New York Times*, 26 January, http://www.nytimes.com/2011/01/30/magazine/30WikiLeaks-t.html?_r=1.

22  Pontin, 'Secrets and Transparency'.

23  'Superinjunctions', *Guardian*, www.guardian.co.uk/law/super injunctions.

24  R. Nygaard, 1998, *In re Madden*, quoted in Y. Benkler, 2011, *A Free Irresponsible Press: WikiLeaks and the Battle over the Soul of the Networked Fourth Estate*, Working Draft, http://benkler.org/Benkler%20WikiLeaks%20CRCL%20Working%20Paper%20Feb_8.pdf, p. 39.

25  Benkler, *A Free Irresponsible Press*.

26  H. Clinton, 2010, Remarks on Internet Freedom, US Department of State, 21 January, www.state.gov/secretary/rm/2010/01/135519.htm.

27  Ibid.

28  H. Clinton, 2011, 'Internet Rights and Wrongs: Choices & Challenges in a Networked World', US Department of State, 15 February, www.state.gov/secretary/rm/2011/02/156619.htm.

29  Ibid.

30  Ibid.

31  G. Greenwald, 2011, 'Applying U.S. Principles on Internet Freedom', *Salon*, 17 January, www.salon.com/news/opinion/glenn_greenwald/2011/01/17/internet/index.html.

32  W. Broad, J. Markoff and D. Sanger, 2011, 'Israeli Test on Worm Called Crucial in Iran Nuclear Delay', *New York Times*, 15 January, www.nytimes.com/2011/01/16/world/middleeast/16stuxnet.html?_r=1.

33  American Civil Liberties Union, 2010, 'Groups Sue over Suspicionless Laptop Search Policy at the Border', ACLU, 7 September, www.aclu.org/free-speech-technology-and-liberty/groups-sue-over-suspicionless-laptop-search-policy-border.

34  H. LaFranchi, 2010, 'US to Federal Workers: If You Read WikiLeaks, You're Breaking the Law', *Christian Science Monitor*, 7 December, www.csmonitor.com/USA/Foreign-Policy/2010/1207/US-to-federal-workers-If-you-read-WikiLeaks-you-re-breaking-the-law.

35  Benkler, 2011, *A Free Irresponsible Press*, http://benkler.org/Benkler%20WikiLeaks%20CRCL%20Working%20Paper%20Feb_8.pdf.

36  '21st Century Statecraft', US Department of State, www.state. gov/statecraft/index.htm.

37  N. Scola, 2010, 'The Che Guevara of 21st Century is the Network', *techPresident*, 19 November, http://techpresident. com/blog-entry/che-guevara-21st-century-network.

38  J. Halliday, 2011, 'Hillary Clinton Advisor Compares Internet to Che Guevera', *Guardian*, 22 June, viewed 23 June, www. guardian.co.uk/media/2011/jun/22/hillary-clinton-adviser-alec-ross?INTCMP=SRCH.

39  '21st Century Statecraft', US Department of State.

40  T. Wu, 2010, *The Master Switch: The Rise and Fall of Information Empires*, New York: Knopf Publishing Group.

41  Ibid., p. 308.

42  Ibid., p. 337.

43  R. MacKinnon, 2010, 'WikiLeaks, Amazon and the New Threat to Internet Speech', *CNN*, 3 December, http://edi tion.cnn.com/2010/OPINION/12/02/mackinnon.WikiLeaks. amazon/.

44  E. Morozov, 2011, *Net Delusion: How Not to Liberate the World*, London: Allen Lane.

45  Ibid., pp. 70–1.

46  Ibid., p. 241.

47  S. Coll, 2011, 'The Internet: For Better or for Worse', *New York Review of Books*, 7 April, www.nybooks.com/articles/ archives/2011/apr/07/internet-better-or-worse/.

48  www.guardian.co.uk/media/2011/mar/15/web-spying-machine -julian-assange.

49  T. Friedman, 2010, 'From WikiChina', *New York Times*, 30 November, www.nytimes.com/2010/12/01/opinion/01fried man.html.

50  R. Godec, 2010, 'US Embassy Cables: Tunisia – A US Foreign Policy Conundrum', *Guardian*, 7 December, www.guardian. co.uk/world/us-embassy-cables-documents/217138.

51  G. Rachman, 2010, 'America Should Give Assange a Medal', *Financial Times*, 13 December, www.ft.com/cms/s/0/61f8fab0-06f3-11e0-8c29-00144feabdc0,s01=1.html#ixzz1E1uaT5SH.

52  I. Black and S. Tisdall, 2010, 'Saudi Arabia Urges US Attack on Iran to Stop Nuclear Programme', *Guardian*, 28 November, www.guardian.co.uk/world/2010/nov/28/us-embassy-cables-

saudis-iran; H. Brooke, 2010, 'WikiLeaks Cables: Saudi Princes Throw Parties Boasting Drink, Drugs and Sex', *Guardian*, 7 December, www.guardian.co.uk/world/2010/dec/07/WikiLeaks-cables-saudi-princes-parties.

53  J. Assange, 2010, 'TIME's Julian Assange Interview: Full Transcript/Audio', *TIME*, 1 December, www.time.com/time/world/article/0,8599,2034040,00.html.

54  Ibid.

55  J. Kampfner, 2010, *Freedom for Sale: How We Made Money and Lost Our Liberty*, London: Simon & Schuster.

56  J. Kampfner, 2011, 'WikiLeaks Turned the Tables on Governments, but the Power Relationship Has Not Changed', *Guardian*, 17 January, www.guardian.co.uk/media/2011/jan/17/WikiLeaks-governments-journalism?CMP=twt_fd.

57  Julian Assange quoted in M. Sifry, 2011, *Wikileaks and the Age of Transparency*, Connecticut: Yale University Press.

58  D. Tambini, 2011, 'Wikileaks Revisited: Is Julian Assange a Straw Man?' *LSE Media Policy Project*, 7 April, http://blogs.lse.ac.uk/mediapolicyproject/2011/04/07/wikileaks-revisited-is-julian-assange-a-straw-man/.

59  JumboLeaks, http://jumboleaks.org/.

60  ThaiLeaks, http://wiki.thaileaks.info/.

61  GlobalLeaks, www.globaleaks.org/.

62  JamiiForums, www.jamiiforums.com/.

63  T. Rhodes, 2011, 'The Internet in East Africa: An Aid or a Weapon?' Committee to Protect Journalists, 17 June, viewed 28 June, www.cpj.org/blog/2011/06/the-internet-in-east-africa-an-aid-or-a-weapon.php?utm_source=twitterfeed&utm_medium=twitter.

64  BrusselsLeaks, viewed 10 December 2010, https://brussels-leaks.com/about.

65  F. Brunton, 2011, 'After WikiLeaks, Us', *The New Everyday*, 4 April , http://mediacommons.futureofthebook.org/tne/pieces/after-WikiLeaks-us.

66  Al Jazeera English, 2011, 'Anonymous and the Global Correction' – Opinion – *The Genius Files*, 17 Februrary, http://thegeniusfilesblog.blogspot.com/2011/02/anonymous-and-global-correction-opinion.html.

67  'LulzSec Hacking Group Announces End to Cyber Attacks',

2011, *BBC News*, 26 June, viewed 26 June, www.bbc.co.uk/news/uk-13918458.

68 M. Jopling, 2011, 074 CDS 11 E – 'Information and National Security', NATO Parliamentary Assembly, June, viewed 30 June,www.nato-pa.int/default.asp?SHORTCUT=2443.

69 J. Assange, 2011, 'Of the People and for the People', *New Statesman*, 4 April, pp. 21–2.

70 Ibid.

71 A. Darnton and M. Kirk, 2011, *Finding Frames: New Ways to Engage the UK Public in Global Poverty*, London: Bond.

72 C. Beckett, 2009, 'NGOs as Gatekeepers to "Local Media": Networked News for Developing Countries', EDS Innovation Research Programme Discussion Paper Series, no. 21, July, pp. 1–12.

73 Ibid.

74 www.timesonline.co.uk/tol/life_and_style/health/article3602694.ece.

75 N. Davies, 2009, *Flat Earth News: An Award-Winning Reporter Exposes Falsehood, Distortion and Propaganda in the Global Media*, London: Random House UK.

76 P. Starr, 2009, 'Goodbye to the Age of Newspapers (Hello to a New Era of Corruption)', *New Republic*, 4 March, viewed 28 June 2011, www.tnr.com/article/goodbye-the-age-newspapers-hello-new-era-corruption?page=1.

77 L. Lynch, 2010, ' "We're Going to Crack the World Open": WikiLeaks and the Future of Investigative Reporting', *Journalism Practice*, 24 March, pp. 1–10.

78 Davis Merritt in J. Rosenberry and B. St John III (eds.), 2010, *Public Journalism 2.0: The Promise and Reality of a Citizen-Engaged Press*, New York: Routledge, p. 29.

79 Rosenberry and St John III (eds.), *Public Journalism 2.0*, p.152.

80 J. Dewey, 1927, *The Public and its Problems*, New York: Holt.

81 Assange, 'Of the People and for the People'.

82 Benkler, *A Free Irresponsible Press*.

83 'The Palestine Papers', *Al Jazeera*, http://english.aljazeera.net/palestinepapers/.

84 G. Carlstrom, 2011, 'Introducing the Palestine Papers', *Al Jazeera*, 23 January, http://english.aljazeera.net/palestinepapers/2011/01/201112214310263628.html.

85  A. Hammond, 2011, 'Gulf Broadcasters Find Red Line in Uprisings', *Reuters*, 14 April, www.reuters.com/article/2011/04/14/us-mideast-protests-media-idUSTRE73D1KD20110414.

86  R. Booth, 'WikiLeaks cables claim al-Jazeera changed coverage to suit Qatari foreign policy', *Guardian*, 6 December 2010, www.guardian.co.uk/world/2010/dec/05/WikiLeaks-cables-al-jazeera-qatari-foreign-policy.

87  'SafeHouse', *Wall Street Journal*, https://www.wsjsafehouse.com/.

### 4  Social media as disruptive journalism: media, politics and network effects

1  'WikiLeaks: Stop the Crackdown', Avaaz, viewed 28 June 2011, https://secure.avaaz.org/en/WikiLeaks_petition/.

2  M. Sifry, 2011, *WikiLeaks, Assange, and Why There's No Turning Back* (exclusive excerpt), Huffington Post, 2 September, www.huffingtonpost.com/micah-sifry/WikiLeaks-assange-micah-sifry_b_820671.html.

3  Y. Benkler, 2011, *A Free Irresponsible Press: WikiLeaks and the Battle over the Soul of the Networked Fourth Estate*, Working Draft, http://benkler.org/Benkler%20WikiLeaks%20CRCL%20Working%20Paper%20Feb_8.pdf.

4  J. Heilemann, 2010, 'Caught in Their Web', *New York*, 12 December, http://nymag.com/news/politics/powergrid/70105/.

5  Report to be published by the Reuters Institute for the Study of Journalism.

6  J. Lloyd, 2011, 'The New Power of the Press', *Financial Times*, 7 January, www.ft.com/cms/s/2/cd68f606-19e0-11e0-b921-0144feab49a.html#axzz1XRlF6Uvv.

7  Ibid.

8  J. Kampfner, 2011, 'WikiLeaks Turned the Tables on Governments, but the Power Relationship Has Not Changed', *Guardian*, 17 January, www.guardian.co.uk/media/2011/jan/17/WikiLeaks-governments-journalism.

9  Ibid.

10  E. Schmidt, and J. Cohen, 2010, 'The Digital Disruption', *Foreign Affairs*, 89.6, November/December, pp. 75-85.

11  Wikipedia, 2011, 'Death of Khaled Mohammed Saeed', 26 June, viewed 26 June 2011, http://en.wikipedia.org/wiki/Khaled_Saeed.

12   Rayanr7, 2011, 'Flash Mob Protesting in Tunis', *YouTube*, 6 January, www.youtube.com/watch?v=NBkOosu6WSs&feature =player_embedded.

13   C. Malin, 2011, 'Strong MENA Interest in Mobile Apps, Spot On Public Relations', 31 January, www.spotonpr.com/strong-mena-interest-in-mobile-apps/.

14   M. Gladwell, 2010, 'Small Change: Why the Revolution Will Not Be Tweeted', *New Yorker*, 4 October, www.newyorker.com/reporting/2010/10/04/101004fa_fact_gladwell#ixzz1PX qPMYtK.

15   'In-depth: WikiLeaks', *Dawn*, www.dawn.com/category/in-depth-WikiLeaks-news.

16   N. Ram, 2011, 'Revealed: The India Cables From WikiLeaks', *Hindu*, 15 March, www.thehindu.com/news/the-india-cables/article1538083.ece.

17   P. Starr, 2009, 'Goodbye to the Age of Newspapers (Hello to a New Era of Corruption)', *The New Republic*, 4 March, viewed 28 June 2011, www.tnr.com/article/goodbye-the-age-newspapers-hello-new-era-corruption?page=1.

18   John Lloyd, 2011, Email to Charlie Beckett, published in C. Beckett, 2011, 'Journalism and Power: The Importance of the Institution', *Polis Blog*, 27 June, http://blogs.lse.ac.uk/polis/2011/06/27/journalism-and-power-the-importance-of-the-inst itution/.

19   A. Rusbridger, 2010, 'The Hugh Cudlipp Lecture: Does Journalism Exist?' *Guardian*, 25 January, www.guardian.co.uk/media/2010/jan/25/cudlipp-lecture-alan-rusbridger.

20   B. Keller, 2011, 'Dealing with Assange and the WikiLeaks Secrets', *New York Times*, 26 January, www.nytimes.com/2011/01/30/magazine/30WikiLeaks-t.html?_r=1.

21   www.bbc.co.uk/news/uk-england-norfolk-13813788.

22   Beckett, 'Journalism and Power'.

23   E. Morozov, 2010, 'Cyber Guerrillas Can Help US', *Financial Times*, 3 December, www.ft.com/cms/s/0/d3dd7c40-ff15-11df-956b-00144feab49a.html#axzz1KupBNk1i.

24   E. Morozov, 2010, 'Why It's Hard to Duplicate', *New York Times* [online], 11 December, www.nytimes.com/roomfordebate/2010/12/09/what-has-WikiLeaks-started/WikiLeaks-relationship-with-the-media.

25  E. Morozov, 2011, 'The Future of WikiLeaks', *RSA*, 20 January, www.thersa.org/events/audio-and-past-events/2011/the-future-of-WikiLeaks.

26  Assange quoted in M. Brian, 2011, 'WikiLeaks Founder: Facebook is the Most Appalling Spy Machine That Has Ever Been Invented', *The Next Web: Facebook*, 2 May, http://thenextweb.com/facebook/2011/05/02/WikiLeaks-founder-facebook-is-the-most-appalling-spy-machine-that-has-ever-been-invented/.

27  J. Assange, 2010, 'TIME's Julian Assange Interview: Full Transcript/Audio', *TIME*, 1 December, www.time.com/time/world/article/0,8599,2034040,00.html.

28  Assange quoted in M. Sifry, 2011, *WikiLeaks and the Age of Transparency*, Connecticut: Yale University Press.

29  M. Beckford, 2010, 'Sarah Palin: Hunt WikiLeaks Founder like al-Qaeda and Taliban Leaders', *Telegraph*, 30 November, www.telegraph.co.uk/news/worldnews/WikiLeaks/8171269/Sarah-Palin-hunt-WikiLeaks-founder-like-al-Qaeda-and-Taliban-leaders.html.

30  S. Valen, 2011, 'Why I Have Nominated WikiLeaks for the Nobel Peace Prize', *Snorre Valen*, 2 February, www.snorrevalen.no/2011/02/02/why-i-have-nominated-WikiLeaks-for-the-nobel-peace-prize/.

31  J. Naughton, in bbccojovideo, 2011, #polis11: 'After WikiLeaks', YouTube, 12 June, viewed 12 June2011, www.youtube.com/watch?feature=player_embedded&v=_ILi1aH5Wj8.

32  G. Lovink and P. Riemens, 2010, 'Ten Theses on WikiLeaks, *Net Critiques* by Geert Lovink', 30 August, http://networkcultures.org/wpmu/geert/2010/08/30/ten-theses-on-WikiLeaks/.

33  Dr Alison Powell, London School of Economics, in bbccojovideo, 2011, #polis11: 'After WikiLeaks', YouTube, 12 June, viewed 12 June 2011, www.youtube.com/watch?feature=player_embedded&v=_ILi1aH5Wj8.

34  A. Galloway and E. Thacker, 2007, *The Exploit: A Theory of Networks*, Minnesota: University of Minnesota Press.

35  C. Anderson, 2010, 'How WikiLeaks Affects Journalism', interviewed by Jayshree Bajoria, Council on Foreign Relations, 29 December, www.cfr.org/terrorism/WikiLeaks-

affects-journalism/p23696; C. Anderson, 2010, 'About Me', C.W.Anderson.org, 13 June, www.cwanderson.org/?p=239.

36  J. O'Loughlin, F. Witmer, A. Linke, and N. Thorwardson, 2010, 'Peering into the Fog of War: The Geography of the WikiLeaks Afghanistan War Logs, 2004–2009', *Eurasian Geography and Economics*, 51.4, pp. 472–95.

37  Professor George Brock, City University, in bbccojovideo, 2011, #polis11: 'After WikiLeaks', YouTube, 12 June, viewed 12 June 2011, www.youtube.com/watch?feature=player_embedded&v=_ILi1aH5Wj8.

38  Angela Philips, Goldsmiths University, in bbccojovideo, 2011, #polis11: 'After WikiLeaks', YouTube, 12 June, viewed 12 June 2011, www.youtube.com/watch?feature=player_embedded&v=_ILi1aH5Wj8.

39  J. Pontin, 2011, 'Secrets and Transparency', *Technology Review*, 26 January, viewed 27 June, 2011, www.technologyreview.com/blog/pontin/26314/?p1=A3.

40  M. Castells, 2009, *Communication Power*, Oxford: Oxford University Press, p. 49.

41  G. Muhlmann, 2008, *A Political History of Journalism*, trans. J. Birrell, Cambridge: Polity Press, p. 259.

42  Ibid., p. 227.

43  C. Shirky, 2010, *WikiLeaks and the Long Haul*, 6 December, www.shirky.com/weblog/2010/12/WikiLeaks-and-the-long-haul/.

44  Anderson, 'How WikiLeaks Affects Journalism'.

45  Lovink. and Riemens, 'Ten Theses on WikiLeaks'.

46  J. Schumpeter, 1967, *Capitalism, Socialism and Democracy*, New York: Harpers.

*Epilogue*

1  http://wikileaks.org/cablegate.html (all notes to the Epilogue cite articles accessed on 4 September 2011 unless otherwise stated).

2  www.wired.com / threatlevel / 2011 / 09 / wikileaks-unredacted-cables.

3  Ibid.

4  www.spiegel.de/international/world/0,1518,783084,00.html. See also http://unspecified.wordpress.com/2011/09/03/wikileaks-password-leak-faq/.

5  D. Leigh and L. Harding, 2011, *WikiLeaks: Inside Julian Assange's War On Secrecy*, London: Guardian Books, ch. 11.
6  www.freitag.de/politik/1134-nerds-ohne-nerven.
7  http://nigelparry.com/news/guardian-david-leigh-cablegate.shtml.
8  www.guardian.co.uk/media/2011/sep/02/wikileaks-publishes-cache-unredacted-cables.
9  http://en.rsf.org/reporters-without-borders-01-09-2011,40905.html.
10  http://techpresident.com/blog-entry/fall-wikileaks-cablegate2-assange-and-icarus.

# BIBLIOGRAPHY

Adler, B., 2011, 'Why Journalists Aren't Standing Up for WikiLeaks', *Newsweek*, 4 January, www.newsweek.com/2011/01/04/why-journalists-aren-t-defending-julian-assange.html#.

Alford, C., 2010, 'Whistle-Blowing, Redefined', *New York Times* [online], 9 January, www.nytimes.com/roomfordebate/2010/12/09/what-has-wikileaks-started/wikileaks-is-no-whistle-blower.

Allan, S., 2006, *Online News: Journalism and the Internet*, Bucks.: Open University Press.

Anderson, R., 2010, 'The Downside of Data Sharing', *New York Times* [online], 10 December, www.nytimes.com/roomfordebate/2010/12/09/what-has-wikileaks-started/data-security-in-the-age-of-wikileaks.

Assange, J. [attributed], 2006, 'Conspiracy as Governance', *Cryptome*, 3 December, http://cryptome.org/0002/ja-conspiracies.pdf.

Assange, J. [attributed], 2010, 'Julian Assange Writes on Cypherpunks, 1995-2002', *Cryptome*, 21 May, http://cryptome.org/0001/assange-cpunks.htm.

Assange, J. [attributed], 2006, 'The Non Linear Effects of Leaks on Unjust Systems of Governance', *Cryptome*, 31 December, http://cryptome.org/0002/ja-conspiracies.pdf.

Assange, J., 2011, 'Of the People and for the People', *New Statesman*, 4 April, pp. 21–2.

Assange, J., 2006, 'The Road to Hanoi', *CounterPunch*, 5 December, www.counterpunch.org/assange12052006.html.

Assange, J., 2010, Speech at the 2010 Oslo Freedom Forum, April, transcript available: www.religiousforums.com/forum/political-debates/01236-transcript-julian-assange-wikileaks-speech-2010-a.html.

Assange, J. [attributed], 2006, 'State and Terrorist Conspiracies', *Cryptome*, 10 November, http://cryptome.org/0002/ja-conspiracies.pdf.

Atton, C., 2002, *Alternative Media*, London: SAGE Publications Ltd.

Bailey, O., Cammaerts, C. and Carpentier, N., 2007, *Understanding Alternative Media*, Bucks.: Open University Press.

Bamford, J., 2010, Forcing Governments to Confess, *New York Times* [online], 9 December, www.nytimes.com/roomfordebate/2010/12/09/what-has-wikileaks-started/wikileaks-shows-that-deception-begets-deception.

bbccojovideo, 2011, #polis11: 'After Wikileaks', *YouTube*, 12 June, viewed 12 June, 2011, www.youtube.com/watch?feature=player_embedded&v=_ILi1aH5Wj8.

Beckett, C., 2009, 'NGOs as Gatekeepers to "Local Media": Networked News for Developing Countries', EDS Innovation Research Programme Discussion Paper Series, no. 21, July, pp. 1–12.

Beckett, C., 2008, *SuperMedia: Saving Journalism So It Can Save the World*, Oxford: Wiley-Blackwell.

Beckett, C., 2010, *The Value of Networked Journalism*, Polis Report, London: London School of Economics.

Bell, E., 2010, 'How WikiLeaks Has Woken Up Journalism', Emily Bell Blog http://emilybellwether.wordpress.com/2010/12/07/how-wikileaks-has-woken-up-journalism/.

Benkler, Y., 2011, *A Free Irresponsible Press: WikiLeaks and the Battle over the Soul of the Networked Fourth Estate*, Working Draft, http://benkler.org/Benkler%20Wikileaks%20CRCL%20Working%20Paper%20Feb_8.pdf.

Benkler, Y., 2006, *The Wealth of Networks: How Social Production Transforms Markets and Freedom*, Connecticut: Yale University Press.

Bernstein, C. and Woodward, B., 1974, *All the President's Men*, New York: Simon & Schuster.

Brian, M., 2011, 'Wikileaks Founder: Facebook is the Most Appalling Spy Machine That Has Ever Been Invented', The Next Web: Facebook, 2 May, http://thenextweb.com/facebook/2011/05/02/wikileaks-founder-facebook-is-the-most-appalling-spy-machine-that-has-ever-been-invented/.

Brunton, F., 2011, 'After WikiLeaks, Us', *The New Everyday*, 4 April, http://mediacommons.futureofthebook.org/tne/pieces/after-wikileaks-us.

Cadwalladr, C., 2010, 'Julian Assange, Monk of the Online Age Who Thrives on Intellectual Battle', *Guardian*, 1 August, www.guardian.co.uk/media/2010/aug/01/julian-assange-wikileaks-afghanistan.

Cardoso, G., 2009, *From Mass Communication to Networked Communication: Thoughts 2.0*, LINI Working Papers, no. 1, pp. 13–45.

Caryl, C., 2011, 'Why WikiLeaks Changes Everything', *New York Review of Books*, 15 January, www.nybooks.com/articles/archives/2011/jan/13/why-wikileaks-changes-everything/.

Castells, M., 2009, *Communication Power*, Oxford: Oxford University Press.

Castells, M., 2000, *The Information Age: Economy, Society, and Culture*, Volume I: *The Rise of the Network Society*, 2nd edn, Oxford: Blackwell Publishers.

Castells, M., 2001, *The Internet Galaxy: Reflections on the Internet, Business, and Society*, Oxford: Oxford University Press.

Chadwick, A. and Howard, P. (eds.), 2009, *Routledge Handbook of Internet Politics*, New York: Routledge.

Coleman, S. and Blumer, J., 2009, *The Internet and Democratic Citizenship: Theory, Practice, and Policy*, New York: Cambridge University Press.

Dahlgren, P., 2009, *Media and Political Engagement*, Cambridge: Cambridge University Press.

Davies, N., 2009, *Flat Earth News: An Award-Winning Reporter Exposes Falsehood, Distortion and Propaganda in the Global Media*, London: Random House UK.

Dewey, J., 1927, *The Public and its Problems*, New York: Holt.

Diebert, R., 2010, 'The Post Cable-Gate Era', *New York Times* [online], 11 December, www.nytimes.com/roomfordebate/2010/12/09/what-has-wikileaks-started/after-wikileaks-a-new-era.

Domscheit-Berg, D., 2011, *Inside Wikileaks: My Time With Julian Assange at the World's Most Dangerous Website*, New York: Crown Publishers.

Downie, L., Jr and Kaiser, R., 2003, *The News about the News*, New York: Random House.

Downie, L., Jr and Shudson, M., 2009, 'Finding a New Model for News Reporting', *Washington Post*, 19 October, p. A19.

Fenton, N. (ed.), 2010, *New Media, Old News: Journalism and Democracy in the Digital Age*, London: SAGE Publications Ltd.

Foster, J. and McChesney, R., 2011, 'The Internet's Unholy Marriage to Capitalism', *Monthly Review*, 62.10, March, http://monthlyreview.org/2011/03/01/the-internets-unholy-marriage-to-capitalism.

Friedman, T., 2010, 'We've Only Got America', *New York Times*, 14 December, www.nytimes.com/2010/12/15/opinion/15friedman.html?_r=1&partner=rssnyt&emc=rss.

Galloway, A., 2004, *Protocol: How Control Exists after Decentralization*, Massachusetts: Massachusetts Institute of Technology Press.

Galloway, A. and Thacker, E., 2007, *The Exploit: A Theory of Networks*, Minnesota: University of Minnesota Press.

Grueskin, B., Seave, A. and Graves, L., 2011, *The Story So Far: What We Know about the Business of Digital Journalism*, New York: Columbia Journalism School.

Hargreaves, I., 2005, *Journalism: A Very Short Introduction*, Oxford: Oxford University Press.

Herman, E. and Chomsky, N., 1988, *Manufacturing Consent: The Political Economy of the Mass Media*, New York: Pantheon.

Hindman, M., 2009, *The Myth of Digital Democracy*, Princeton, NJ: Princeton University Press.

Jenkins, H., 2008, *Convergence Culture: Where Old and New Media Collide*, New York: New York University Press.

Kampfner, J., 2010, *Freedom for Sale: How We Made Money and Lost Our Liberty*, London: Simon & Schuster.

Keller, B., 2011, 'Dealing with Assange and the WikiLeaks Secrets', *New York Times*, 6 January, www.nytimes.com/2011/01/30/magazine/30Wikileaks-t.html?_r=1.

Khatchadourian, R., 2010, 'No Secrets', *New Yorker*, 7 June, www.

newyorker.com/reporting/2010/06/07/100607fa_fact_khatchado
urian?printable=true.

Lanier, J., 2010, 'The Hazards of Nerd Supremacy: The Case of
WikiLeaks', *Atlantic*, 20 December, www.theatlantic.com/tech
nology/archive/2010/12/the-hazards-of-nerd-supremacy-the-case
-of-wikileaks/68217/.

Leigh, D. and Harding, L., 2011, *WikiLeaks: Inside Julian Assange's
War on Secrecy*, London: Guardian Books.

Lessig, L., 2003, *The Future of Ideas: The Fate of the Commons in a
Connected World*, New York: Random House.

Lippman, W., 1922, *Public Opinion*, New York: Free Press.

Lloyd, J., 2011, 'The New Power of the Press', *Financial Times*, 7
January, www.ft.com/cms/s/2/cd68f606-19e0-11e0-b921-00144
feab49a.html#axzz1XRlF6Uvv.

Lloyd, J., 2004, *What the Media are Doing to Our Politics*, London:
Constable & Robinson.

Lovink, G. and Riemens, P., 2010, 'Ten Theses on Wikileaks, *Net
Critiques* by Geert Lovink', 30 August, http://networkcultures.
org/wpmu/geert/2010/08/30/ten-theses-on-wikileaks/.

McGreal, C., 2010, 'Wikileaks Reveals Video Showing US Air Crew
Shooting Down Iraqi Citizens', *Guardian*, 5 April, www.guardian.
co.uk/world/2010/apr/05/wikileaks-us-army-iraq-attack.

Monck, A., 2008, *Can You Trust the Media?* Cambridge: Icon
Books.

Morozov, E., 2011, *Net Delusion: How Not to Liberate the World*,
London: Allen Lane.

Morozov, E., 2010, 'Why It's Hard to Duplicate', *New York Times*
[online], 11 December, www.nytimes.com/roomfordebate/2010/
12/09/what-has-wikileaks-started/wikileaks-relationship-with-th
e-media.

Muhlmann, G., 2008, *A Political History of Journalism*, trans.
J. Birrell, Cambridge: Polity Press.

Naughton, J., 2010, 'WikiLeaks Row: Why Amazon's Desertion
Has Ominous Implications for Democracy', *Guardian*, 11
December, www.guardian.co.uk/technology/2010/dec/11/wiki
leaks-amazon-denial-democracy-lieberman.

*New Statesman*, 2011, 'Assange: "WikiLeaks is the intelligence
agency of the people"', The Staggers, 5 April, www.newstates
man.com/blogs/the-staggers/2011/04/assange-wikileaks-radical.

O'Loughlin, J., Witmer, F., Linke, A. and Thorwardson, N., 2010, 'Peering into the Fog of War: The Geography of the WikiLeaks Afghanistan War Logs, 2004–2009', *Eurasian Geography and Economics*, 51.4, pp. 472–95.

Papacharissi, Z., 2010, *A Private Sphere: Democracy in a Digital Age*, Cambridge: Polity Press.

Papacharissi, Z. (ed.), 2009, *Journalism and Citizenship: New Agendas in Communication*, New York: Routledge.

Pontin, J., 2011, 'Secrets and Transparency', *Technology Review*, 26 January, viewed 27 June 2011, www.technologyreview.com/blog/pontin/26314/?p1=A3.

Powell, A., 2011, 'The WikiLeaks Phenomenon and New Media Power', *The New Everyday*, 8 April, http://mediacommons.futureofthebook.org / tne / pieces / wikileaks-phenomenon-and-new-media-power.

Rachman, G., 2010, 'America Should Give Assange a Medal', *Financial Times*, 13 December, www.ft.com/cms/s/0/61f8fab0-06f3-11e0-8c29-00144feabdc0,s01=1.html#ixzz1E1uaT5SH.

Rantanen, T., 2009, *When News Was New*, Oxford: Wiley-Blackwell.

Rosanvallon, P., 2008, *Counter-Democracy: Politics in an Age of Distrust*, trans. A. Goldhammer, Cambridge: Cambridge University Press.

Rosen, J., 2001, *What Are Journalists For?* Connecticut: Yale University Press.

Rosenberry, J. and St John III, B. (eds.), 2010, *Public Journalism 2.0: The Promise and Reality of a Citizen-Engaged Press*, New York: Routledge.

Rusbridger, A., 2010, 'The Hugh Cudlipp Lecture: Does Journalism Exist?' *Guardian*, 25 January, www.guardian.co.uk/media/2010/jan/25/cudlipp-lecture-alan-rusbridger.

Sanger, L., 2010, 'A Comment on WikiLeaks', *LarrySanger.org*, 29 November, www.larrysanger.org/wikileaks.html.

Schudson, M., 2011, *The Good Citizen: A History of American Civic Life*, New York: Free Press.

Schudson, M., 2008, *Why Democracies Need an Unlovable Press*, Cambridge: Polity Press.

Schumpeter, J., 2010, *Capitalism, Socialism, and Democracy*, Oxford: Routledge.

Shirky, C., 2009, *Here Comes Everybody: How Change Happens When People Come Together*, London: Penguin Books.

Shirky, C., 2010, 'Wikileaks and the Long Haul', *Clay Shirky*, 6 December, www.shirky.com/weblog/2010/12/wikileaks-and-the-long-haul/.

Sifry, M., 2011, *Wikileaks and the Age of Transparency*, Connecticut: Yale University Press.

Starr, P., 2004, *The Creation of the Media: Political Origins of Modern Communications*, New York: Basic Books.

Starr, P., 2009, 'Goodbye to the Age of Newspapers (Hello to a New Era of Corruption)', *The New Republic*, 4 March, viewed 28 June 2011, www.tnr.com/article/goodbye-the-age-newspapers-hello-new-era-corruption?page=1.

Tambini, D., 2011, 'Wikileaks Revisited: Is Julian Assange a Straw Man?' *LSE Media Policy Project*, 7 April, http://blogs.lse.ac.uk/mediapolicyproject/2011/04/07/wikileaks-revisited-is-julian-assange-a-straw-man/.

Tumber, H. (ed.), 2000, *News: A Reader*, Oxford: Oxford University Press.

Tunney, S. and Monaghan, G. (eds.), 2009, *Web Journalism: A New Form of Citizenship?* East Sussex: Sussex Academic Press.

Ugland, E. and Henderson, J., 2007, 'Who Is a Journalist and Why Does it Matter? Disentangling the Legal and Ethical Arguments', *Journal of Mass Media Ethics*, 22.4, October, pp. 241–61.

WikiLeaks, 2010, *Collateral Murder*, 6 July, www.collateralmurder.com.

Wikipedia, 2011, 'Information Published by WikiLeaks', 15 June, viewed 16 June 2011, http://en.wikipedia.org/wiki/Information_published_by_WikiLeaks.

Wu, T., 2010, *The Master Switch: The Rise and Fall of Information Empires*, New York: Knopf Publishing Group.

Zelizer, B., 2004, *Taking Journalism Seriously: News and the Academy*, Thousand Oaks, CA: SAGE Publications, Inc.

*Interviews with Assange*

Assange, J., 2010, 'Julian Assange Answers Your Questions', *Guardian*, 3 December, www.guardian.co.uk/world/blog/2010/dec/03/julian-assange-wikileaks.

Assange, J., 2010, 'TIME's Julian Assange Interview: Full

Transcript/Audio', *TIME*, 1 December, www.time.com/time/ world/article/0,8599,2034040,00.html.

Assange, J., 2010, 'WikiLeaks Founder Julian Assange on the "War Logs"', *SPIEGEL*, 26 July, www.spiegel.de/international/world/ 0,1518,708518,00.html.

Beckow, S., 2011, 'Transcript: Julian Assange Interviewed by CBS *60 Minutes'* Steve Kroft', *The 2010 Scenario*, 1 February, http:// stevebeckow.com/2011/02/transcript-julian-assange-interviewed -cbs-60-minutes-steve-kroft/.

Greenberg, A., 2010, 'An Interview with WikiLeaks' Julian Assange', *Forbes*, 29 November, http://blogs.forbes.com/andy greenberg/2010/11/29/an-interview-with-wikileaks-julian-assan ge/5/.

Greg Mitchell writes a daily blog that scrapes references to WikiLeaks: www.thenation.com/blogs/media-fix.

# INDEX